Ann Arbor Criminal Defense Playbook

Jonathan A. Paul, Esq.

DEDICATION

To My Kids

TABLE OF CONTENTS

CHAPTER ONE

WASHTENAW COUNTY OVERVIEW

Washtenaw County is a unique place to practice law due to the population fluctuation from the University of Michigan, and hosting seven to eight college football games every fall. The 2010 census population for the County was 344,791, but that does not account for the approximate 45,000 undergraduate and graduate students, and the 110,000 visitors on a football Saturday. This means that at one time, there could be half a million people in the County, with a good portion of those people gathered within a mile or two radius in Downtown Ann Arbor.

These factors lend themselves to a lot of out of towners charged with crimes, along with college-aged students who are barely moved out of their parents homes, and thousands of miles away. I'd say forty percent of my Washtenaw County practice involves either a University of Michigan student or an out of town visitor. I spend a lot of time explaining the process to the client, even more than if the client is from the area, and somewhat familiar with the process.

Simple questions like, "where is the courthouse?", or "is this really a misdemeanor, because it's a civil infraction in my state?" are frequent questions I hear. I also spend a lot of time speaking to parents, spouses, and family members and friends, because the client requests that a third party be involved in the process when selecting an attorney. It's my goal to educate the potential client on their Washtenaw County case, and make sure they understand the process from day one. I expect active participation from my client, and I am very selective in who I agree to represent. I will breakdown my proactive program later in this book, and go into greater detail about the process and its components, but here is how I would generally breakdown Washtenaw County to a new client in six different important parts:

Part One

If you're charged with a misdemeanor, this part does not apply, but it's important to either focus on this distinction if you're charged with a felony, or take it off the table for a client. If you're charged with a misdemeanor, you can advance forward, if you're charged with a felony, this is an important concept to understand.

All felonies in Washtenaw County are handled at the 22nd Circuit Court, which is located at 101 East Huron Street, which is located downtown right off Main Street. It's an older court building north of all the downtown restaurants, and for criminal matters, all juvenile cases and felony cases that have been bound over from the district court level are handled in this building. If you're under 16 years old, regardless of the level of the offense, your case will be in this building. This courthouse also handles domestic, civil and business cases. Do not confuse this courthouse with the newer courthouse further down the street at 301 East Huron Street, which is the 15th District Court.

The 22nd Circuit Court is the last stop for felonies, as all felonies begin at the 14A-1 Court for arraignment, Preliminary Examination Conference and Preliminary Examination. The 22nd Circuit Court handles the Pre-Trial, Motion Hearing, Evidentiary Hearing, Final Pretrial, Trial and Sentencing. Once you're at the 22nd Circuit Court, you're knee deep in your case and likely preparing for trial or last minute resolution (more on this later). You will not return to the District Court level unless your case is remanded back by the Circuit Court Judge for a number of reasons, but this is not the common outcome for most felonies already at the Circuit Court level.

Part Two

Washtenaw County has multiple district courts, which are located all around the County. Each district court handles cases for different cities and townships, which will be discussed in greater detail later in this book, but for overview purposes, here are the locations of the district courts.

- Ann Arbor - 15th District Court
- Pittsfield Township - 14A-1 District Court
- City of Ypsilanti - 14A-2 District Court
- Chelsea - 14A-3 District Court
- Saline - 14A-4 District Court
- Ypsilanti Township - 14-B District Court

If you're charged with a misdemeanor, your case will be handled in one of the district courts. If you're charged with a felony, your preliminary examination proceedings (more on this later), will be held at the 14A-1 District Court in Pittsfield Township before heading to the Circuit Court. Misdemeanor cases will not go to the Circuit Court, or any of the district courts, and the judge will remain the same.

Part Three

In Washtenaw County, the process of being charged with a crime is always the same, except for "ticket cases" which I will discuss later on.

For the most part, the client makes contact with a police officer either immediately after the alleged offense occurred, during the offense, or days or weeks later. An alleged victim and/or eyewitnesses may be involved prior to this contact, but ultimately the police and the client make some sort of contact. From there, the police department will write up a report, and if the facts are warranted for review, the police department will submit the case to a prosecutor who will review the facts of the case, and determine if this person should be charged, and if so, what charges. This hand-over from the police to the prosecutor could be within 24 hours or multiple months, depending upon the extent of the investigation.

If the prosecutor determines that charges are warranted, they will submit a warrant to a judge to review and sign, and the client becomes officially charged with a crime(s). If it's a felony, an arrest warrant will be issued, and the client could be arrested at any time. If the charge is a misdemeanor, an arrest warrant can be issued or a notice will be sent in the mail to the client, and an attorney if the client has hired one.

It is quite common for a police officer to submit the facts of a case to the prosecutor, which results in the prosecutor telling the police officer that he/she needs further investigation before a decision can be made. In the prosecutor world this is called "furthered". This means that at the present time, the prosecutor does not have enough to submit charges, and the police officer is given the task of filling in the missing information. If after additional investigation is conducted, the prosecutor can deny the charges or proceed with prosecution.

In a "ticket case", which is more common in Ann Arbor than other part of the County, the police officer will issue a ticket on the spot, and there will be a time period where the client must turn themselves into the court or a bench warrant can be issued for their arrest. This skips the step of the prosecutor and judge reviewing the case, and speeds up the process, which can be quite alarming for a student or someone who is leaving town with no immediate plans to return to the County (more on this process later). The key to a ticket case is calling a timeout, slowing things down, and putting a comprehensive plan in place to resolve your case in a favorable way.

Part Four

Depending on your charge, your case may be handled by the Washtenaw County Prosecutor's Office or a local city or township prosecutor. This is one of the most important distinctions to identify at the beginning of your case. The Washtenaw County Prosecutor's Office handles cases county wide, including all felonies, second and third offense drunk driving cases, the majority of domestic violence cases, and some other repeat offender cases. Most first offense crimes, including drunk driving, retail fraud, possession of marijuana, minor in possession, and other similar offenses are handled by the city or township prosecutor.

These distinctions do not apply if the arresting police agency is Michigan State Police, Washtenaw County Sheriff's Office, University of Michigan Police Department or some other agencies, because these are state agencies, and the case must go to the Washtenaw County Prosecutor's Office, and not the localized prosecutor. More on which prosecutor is better for your case later in this book.

In general, the Washtenaw County Prosecutor's Office will take more time to review and prosecute a case, whereas the local prosecutor such as the Ann Arbor City Prosecutor may prosecute the Monday after your weekend run-in with the law.

If you're under investigation for a crime, it is likely that the Washtenaw County Prosecutor's Office is the prosecutor in your case, as the local prosecutors charge without much of an investigation.

Part Five

As noted above, there are a lot of police agencies in Washtenaw County who may be involved in your case. The policy agency may not only determine which prosecutor handles your case, but could be the determining factor in charges being submitted or not. I know some police agencies in the County that are more likely to cut someone a break vs other agencies which are not as generous with their decision making process.

Determining the police agency is important, because police reports, videos, audio, and other records relevant to your case are held by the police department. Some police departments are better about making discovery available sooner than others, and preserving all evidence. Here is a list of all the police agencies that submit cases for Washtenaw County:

- Michigan State Police (Jackson, Brighton & Monroe)
- Washtenaw County Sheriff's Office
- Ann Arbor Police Department
- Chelsea Police Department

- Eastern Michigan University Police Department
- Milan Police Department
- Ypsilanti Police Department
- University of Michigan Police Department
- Pittsfield Township Police Department
- Saline Police Department
- Northfield Township Police Department

Here is a list of all the current prosecutors in Washtenaw County

State Prosecutor

Washtenaw County Prosecuting Attorney

Brian Mackie

200 N. Main

Ann Arbor, MI 48108

(734) 222-6620

City Prosecutors

City of Ann Arbor
Stephen K. Postema
301 E. Huron
Third Floor
Ann Arbor, MI 48107

Chelsea City

Jeffrey D. Alber

119 S. Main St.

PO Box 440

Chelsea, MI 48118

Milan City

Jesse O'Jack

PO Box 363 St

Saline, MI 48176

Saline City

Dickinson Wright PLC

Doron Yitzchaki

350 S. Main St. Ste 300

Ann Arbor, MI 48104

Ypsilanti City

John Barr

105 Pearl St.

Ypsilanti, MI 48197

Township Prosecutors

Ann Arbor Township

Stefani Carter

4007 Carpenter Rd., #24

Ypsilanti, MI 48197

Augusta Township

Rolland Sizemore

302 N. Huron St.

Ypsilanti, MI 48197

Bridgewater Township
Bruce Laidlaw
2023 Vinewood
Ann Arbor, MI 48104

Dexter Township
Peter Flintoft
119 S. Main St.
Chelsea, MI 48118
(734) 475-8671

Freedom Township
Victor Lillich
101 N. Main, Suite 575
Ann Arbor, MI 48104

Lima Township
Victor Lillich
101 N. Main, Suite 575
Ann Arbor, MI 48104

Lodi Township
Jesse O'Jack
PO Box 363
Saline, MI 48176

Lyndon Township
Peter Flintoft
119 S. Main St.
Chelsea, MI 48118
(734) 475-8671

Manchester Township
Bruce Laidlaw
2023 Vinewood
Ann Arbor, MI 48104
(734) 663-3481

Northfield Township
Paul Burns
133 W. Grand River Ave.
Brighton, MI 48116
(810) 227-5000

Pittsfield Township
James Fink
320 N. Main, Suite 300
Ann Arbor, MI 48104
(734) 994-1077

Salem Township
Holly Battersby
34405 W. 12 Mile Rd., Suite 200
Farmington Hills, MI 48331
(248) 489-4100

Saline Township
Victor Lillich
101 N. Main, Suite 575
Ann Arbor, MI 48104
(734) 769-9050

Scio Township
Victor Lillich
101 N. Main, Suite 575
Ann Arbor, MI 48104
(734) 769-9050

Superior Township
Victor Lillich
101 N. Main, Suite 575
Ann Arbor, MI 48104

Sylvan Township
Peter Flintoft
119 S. Main St.
Chelsea, MI 48118

Webster Township
Victor Lillich
101 N. Main, Suite 575
Ann Arbor, MI 48104

York Township
Victor Lillich
101 N. Main, Suite 575
Ann Arbor, MI 48104

Village Prosecutors

Barton Hills Village
Victor Lillich
101 N. Main, Suite 575
Ann Arbor, MI 48104

Dexter Village
Tom Stringer
320 N. Main St. Suite 100
Ann Arbor, MI 48104

Manchester Village
Victor Lillich
101 N. Main, Suite 575
Ann Arbor, MI 48104

Part Six

Once the police department has been determined, the prosecutor is identified, and you know which courthouse to go to, now comes the next question: who will be my judge? In Washtenaw County, there are four different categories of judges.

The first category is the Circuit Court judges who are elected countywide, but could handle all different types of matters, such as domestic, civil, business and criminal law cases. The role of these judges vary by year, and roles can be changed due to the changing needs of the Circuit Court. As of the Summer of 2015, the current judges at the 22nd Circuit Court who are handling criminal cases are the following:

- Honorable Archie C. Brown
- Honorable Carol Kuhnke
- Honorable Darlene A. O'Brien
- Honorable David S. Swartz

This list will change in the future, but as of the publication of this book, if you are charged with a felony, you will have one of these four judges assigned to your case. As discussed earlier, if you're charged with a felony, you will not see this judge immediately. All felonies in the County are first handled at the 14A-1 Court in Pittsfield Township for arraignments. Preliminary Examination Conference and Preliminary Examination (more on this later). If your case is bound over to the Circuit Court, you will then appear in front of one of these four judges.

The second category of judges are the Ann Arbor 15th District Court judges. These judges handle all criminal misdemeanor cases in Ann Arbor along with participating as rotating judges for the 14A-1 preliminary matters for felonies. A lot of cases in Ann Arbor actually begin with the magistrate, and not the Ann Arbor judges, but with an attorney, you would be able to skip the magistrate level. The current judges in Ann Arbor as of the publication of this book are the following:

- The Honorable Elizabeth Pollard Hines
- The Honorable Karen Valvo
- The Honorable Joseph F. Burke

I will discuss each judge in greater detail later in this book, along with how criminal cases are currently assigned at the 15th District Court.

The third category of judges is the 14A District Court system, which has four different courthouses located in Pittsfield Township, City of Ypsilanti, Chelsea and Saline. These judges rotate frequently, but have been pretty stable over the years: The current judges as of this publication are the following:

- The Honorable Kirk W. Tabbey
- The Honorable Richard E. Conlin
- The Honorable Cedric Simpson

As of this publication, Judge Tabbey handles the 14A-2 District Court dockets, Judge Conlin handles the 14A-1 and 14A-3 dockets, and Judge Simpson handles the 14A-4 dockets. All three judges also rotate within the 14A-1 Preliminary Examination felony system.

The final category is the 14B Charter Township of Ypsilanti court, which is currently handled by Judge Charles Pope who is the elected judge; Judge Pope handles all misdemeanor cases. arraignments and some other traffic and civil matters are handled by Magistrate Mark W. Nelson. This court should not be confused with the 14A-2 Court, which handles City of Ypsilanti cases, which is a completely different courthouse.

Now that we've done a general overview of Washtenaw County, let's jump into more detail about the different courts, judges, common offenses and in my opinion, the best way to handle these cases.

Chapter Two

Washtenaw County 22nd Circuit Court

As discussed in my general overview of the 22nd Circuit Court, there are currently four judges actively being assigned criminal cases. Some of these judges also handle domestic, civil and business cases, but all four judges have dedicated criminal law dockets that they handle weekly. Before we get into more detail about the judges and what happens with your case at the Washtenaw Circuit Court, let's talk about how we even get to this point.

I'm going to use two different examples of cases, as each starts in a different way, but can go in a number of different directions in relation to the Washtenaw Circuit Court. If you're charged with a felony in Washtenaw County, your case is likely follow one of these paths.

Client - Michael - 25 Years Old - Malicious Destruction of Property

Our client Michael was recently arrested for smashing his friend's car with a baseball bat. The alleged incident happened in the City of Saline, and the Washtenaw County Sheriff's Office was the arresting agency. The police arrive on scene to see Michael actively smashing the car and yelling at his friend to "come outside and, let's settle this right now".

The police quickly apprehend Michael, arrest him, and bring him the Washtenaw County Sheriff's Office on Hogback Road for processing. The police will attempt to interview the owner of the car, learn more about what lead to this incident, and attempt to interview Michael about what happened. Michael at this point should be given his *Miranda* rights and should probably not make any statements until he speaks with an attorney.

In our case, the police determine that the damage exceeds $1,000, and this appears to be a felony Malicious Destruction of Property, because the value is above $1,000; if the value was below that level, this would likely be a misdemeanor. Because of the day of the week and the time, the police tell Michael that he can't be released until he sees a judge.

The police gather their information and submit a warrant for Malicious Destruction of Property over $1,000, but below $20,000, and Michael spends the night in jail. The prosecutor in this case will be the Washtenaw County Prosecutor's Office, because it is a felony.

The Washtenaw County Prosecutor's Office will charge Michael immediately if they have enough of a case; if the prosecutor doesn't yet have enough, they may not charge yet, and the case would be furthered for additional information; Michael would then be released pending a warrant.

If Michael is charged, he will likely try to reach out to family and friends, and tell them to contact an attorney to appear at his arraignment, or he may have to be arraigned without an attorney. Michael will not likely see a an actual judge but rather a magistrate; this arraignment will happen at the 14A-1 District Court on Hogback and Washtenaw in Pittsfield Township.

The magistrate will review the current charges, prior criminal history and other bond factors, such as ties to the community and determine what if any bond needs to be posted to assure the safety of the community, and to make sure that Michael returns to the court.

In our case, Michael's family retains an attorney and that attorney is able to appear at the arraignment the next day. The attorney argues that Michael is a first offender, works in Saline, and has the support of his mother, father and brother in the courtroom. The attorney also argues that Michael and his family have invested in the case by hiring an attorney, and look forward to learning more about the case and Michael's options to resolve it.

At this point, the attorney knows very little about the case other than the charge, and may just have have met Michael for the first time. If a magistrate is leaning toward setting a high bond, the attorney may suggest alternative options such as a tether or if drugs and alcohol are a concern, for Michael to test with the Washtenaw County Community Corrections.

A good attorney in Washtenaw County will anticipate what the judge, or in this case, the magistrate may have concerns about, and address them immediately. Because the attorney in this case learns that consumption of high levels of alcohol were involved in this case, Michael's attorney suggest that he be released on a personal bond, but submit to random alcohol or drug testing or if the court sees fit daily testing. Fortunately for Michael, the magistrate grants a personal bond with the condition of daily alcohol testing.

As for all felony cases in Washtenaw County, the magistrate sets two court dates at this time for Michael's case: Preliminary Examination Conference and the Preliminary Examination.

The magistrate sets a date for a Preliminary Examination Conference to be held not less than 7 days or more than 14 days after the date of the arraignment, and a date for a Preliminary Examination of not less than 5 days or more than 7 days after the date of the Preliminary Examination Conference. The dates for the probable cause conference. The Preliminary Examination Conference shall include the following:

(a) Discussions as to a possible plea agreement among the prosecuting attorney, the defendant, and the attorney for the defendant.
(b) Discussions regarding bail and the opportunity for the defendant to petition the magistrate for a bond modification.
(c) Discussions regarding stipulations and procedural aspects of the case.
(d) Discussions regarding any other matters relevant to the case as agreed upon by both parties.

Michael, his family and the attorney are now done with court. Michael will be processed out of the jail, and will see his family in a few hours. From here, the attorney will get to work on the information gathering process of obtaining all available evidence on this case to get the entire picture of all possible defenses for his client. I call this process the information gathering stage.

Michael and his attorney will meet prior to the next court date to review these materials and discuss how to put Michael in the best position during his case. I will discuss this part in detail in my "Winning - A Proactive Approach" section of this book.

Let's keep forward to the next court date, which is called the Preliminary Examination Conference, which is now mandatory in Michigan. This is an opportunity for Michael's attorney and the prosecutor to discuss the case and possible resolutions. At this point the case can go a number of ways:

Option #1 - The client executes a waiver of the 21-day rule, which does not waive the right to preliminary examination (more on this later), but simply waives the right to hold it within 21 days of the arraignment. This allows more time for gathering discovery and negotiation with the prosecutor. If Michael were still in jail due to a very high bond or other holds, it is less likely that this would be waived. Since Michael is out on bond, it would be common to execute this waiver to simply take more time to learn more about the case, and create more options.

Option #2 - The client as stated above is still in jail, and no waiver is executed. This likely means that in a week or two, a preliminary examination would be held at the courthouse where the case would either be dismissed or bound over to the 22nd Circuit Court.

Option #3 - Michael's attorney and the prosecutor have a fruitful conversation and a plea agreement can be worked out on the spot. A possible resolution could be a dismissal of the felony with an agreement to a misdemeanor offense. Michael and his attorney at this point have already discussed this option, and have a plan in place for this outcome.

At this point depending upon, which path is selected, the case will either come back to the same courthouse under Option #1 for another Preliminary Examination Conference, but with additional time to sort things, Option #2, which testimony will be taken by the prosecutor at the Preliminary Examination and the case will either be dismissed or proceed to the 22nd Circuit Court or Option #3, a plea will be taken, and the case will go back to the district court level, which in this case would be the 14A-4 District Court in Saline.

If a Preliminary Examination is held, it is possible that it doesn't end in one day; testimony may be carried over to a second, third or as many court dates as necessary to complete testimony.

If we're proceeding with Option #3, the case never goes to the Washtenaw County Circuit Court. Option #1 could turn into an Option #3 plea agreement or could end up being like Option #2 with a Preliminary Examination to decide the fate of the charges.

Another option not mentioned is the waiver of the Preliminary Examination altogether, not only the 21-day rule, but both sides agreeing not to hold a Preliminary Examination. Both sides must agree on this, and the most common reason is the matter is better handled at the 22nd Circuit Court for resolution.

Michael and his attorney would discuss the pro and cons of all of these options. The case would end up at the 22nd Circuit Court if the Preliminary Examination is held and the case is bound over by the judge, or if both sides waive the Examination, the case will proceed to the Washtenaw County Circuit Court.

Fortunately for Michael, his attorney put him on a proactive program from day one, and was able to negotiate a dismissal agreement with the prosecutor. The prosecutor agreed to dismiss the felony Malicious Destruction of Property and agreed to a misdemeanor, which resulted in the case being sent back to the 14-A4 District Court with Judge Simpson for sentencing. The best way to work toward a reduction in a Malicious Destruction of Property case is being able to pay restitution, and using it as leverage to get the dismissal. The prosecutor is able to make their victim whole, and the client doesn't get a felony on their record.

Example Two - Jennifer - 35 Years - Drunk Driving Third Offense

Our client Jennifer was pulled over for speeding in downtown Ann Arbor by the Ann Arbor Police Department, and upon further investigation, was suspected of drunk driving.

Jennifer refused to take all field sobriety tests, refused the preliminary breath test, and when driven to the station refused to take the DataMaster test. We will get into greater detail on drunk driving cases later in this book, but for purposes of this example, Jennifer was then brought to the hospital where her blood was drawn, and then was released from custody once she no longer had alcohol in her system.

In Michigan, blood results, even in felony cases could take weeks or months to determine, so the police department simply keeps the client in custody until their blood alcohol level reaches 0.00. The client is told that charges will be issued pending the results of the blood test. If there are other charges, such as Reckless Driving or Resisting Arrest, you could be charged with these now, and be charged with the DUI at a later date.

During this time, Jennifer is strongly advised to contact an attorney because of Implied Consent Issues (more on this later), and she should begin a proactive program during this waiting period. It is quite rare that the blood results come back below the legal limit, and even if they do, most prosecutors will still charge the case under the theory of retrograde extrapolation, which introduces evidence that at the time of driving, the client's blood alcohol content was above the legal limit, but went below the legal limit sometime between driving and the blood draw at the hospital.

This example is different than Michael's example above, because Michael was kept in custody to see a judge the next morning, because the police had enough evidence to issue the charges immediately. Things happened quickly for Michael and he had to act immediately. His case was processed immediately, and he may had three to four court appearances within a month.

In Jennifer's example, she is likely to wait at least a month before anything happens. In her case, the police are waiting on results, and once they get the results back, the case will be submitted to the Washtenaw County Prosecutor's Office for review and warrant. Let's assume the blood results come back at 0.11, and the prosecutor identifies two prior drunk driving offenses (more on this later). Jennifer will be charged with Operating While Intoxicated - Third Offense, which is a felony in Michigan.

In our case, Jennifer was smart to hire an attorney immediately who protected her Implied Consent rights, and kept her driver's license appeal rights alive. Because her attorney was tracking her case everyday to see if a warrant has been issued, Jennifer is able to avoid an embarrassing arrest while at work, or at home with her family. If Jennifer had not engaged an attorney immediately, her license would likely be gone for at least the next year with six points on her driving record without even being charged with a ctime.

Jennifer and her attorney would schedule what is called a walk-in arraignment at the 14A-1 District Court, and was able to avoid the embarrassment of an unsuspected arrest. The magistrate was impressed that she tracked her case, and came to court without needing the police to bring her in.

At this point Jennifer has been following her attorney's proactive program for weeks, has alcohol testing in place, and is already in counseling and attending AA meetings. When Jennifer appears before the judge to voluntarily cancel the bench warrant with a proactive plan in place, she is likely to receive a personal bond, and continue what she is already doing in terms of testing and counseling during the case.

Jennifer, like Michael will now proceed down the same path of various court dates, with the same options on the table. Jennifer's example ended up being similar to Michael, because she was aware of the warrant immediately and went to court with her lawyer. Without taking this approach, Jennifer was likely to be surprised by the warrant, and arrested during a minor traffic stop or at the airport while traveling. The warrant is made available to the federal government, and all local governments around the country.

If Jennifer did not turn herself in, she would be brought in front of the judge as a fugitive, who was running for the law (whether true or not). She is likely to have to post a significant monetary bond for her freedom, and will likely spend weeks in the Washtenaw County Jail with a pending case. In this situation, she would not be afforded the luxury of calling a timeout on her case, because she is not free to work, take care of her kids and family, and she simply wants to sprint to some kind of end result in her case, because she is desperate to get out of jail.

We explored all of the options beyond the arraignment for Michael; those same options will apply to Jennifer. Let's assume in this example, the Preliminary Examination is held in Jennifer's case, because the prosecutor is not willing to make any plea offer to Jennifer, and her attorney was not willing to waive the Preliminary Examination. After hearing the evidence, the judge decides to bind the case over the Washtenaw Circuit Court. In Washtenaw County, the judge will tell you when your first court date will be at the Circuit Court and confirm the judge handling the case. The Circuit Court date is typically 4-6 weeks after the last court date at the District Court.

What Happens at the Circuit Court?

Now that we've made it to the Washtenaw County Circuit Court with Jennifer's example, about 4-6 weeks have passed, and her attorney has conducted additional investigation into the facts of the case, and kept an open line of communication with the prosecutor. Jennifer's attorney has started preparing for trial in order to keep a viable option on the table.

The name of the first court date at the Circuit Court is a Pretrial Conference; there is no testimony, trial, guilt or innocence determination, or anything other than somewhat of a status update on the case. Your attorney and the prosecutor handling the case have likely had some conversation about the case before court, and this court date is to bring the judge up to speed on things.

The 22nd Circuit Court feels more formal, because it is; serious felonies are handled in this building and the stakes are higher. Depending upon which judge is assigned to your case, your attorney will check-in with the court staff, and the cases are called on a first-come first-serve basis with limited exceptions. Your attorney should be motivated to be one of the first attorneys to arrive so they can garner the full attention of the prosecutor when they arrive, and have first crack at speaking to the judge.

At the Pretrial Conference, your attorney is likely to “approach” the judge with the prosecutor and have a conference “off the record”. The conversation is quite useful to all parties as both the attorneys and the judge can speak a bit more directly about things without being part of the public record. Common topics are setting a case for trial, a motion or evidentiary hearing, requesting an adjournment or working out a sentencing agreement with the judge.

Once a case is at the felony level at the 22nd Circuit Court, a reduction down to a misdemeanor is quite rare, so a client is faced with filing motions to have the case dismissed, going to trial or pleading guilty or no-contest, but with a sentencing agreement in place. At the felony level, prison time is on the table along with a strong likelihood of jail.

You and your attorney may set a goal to avoid prison time or jail, and be granted probation. This off the record conversation can test those waters with the judge, and possibly gain an agreement with the judge and prosecutor on the sentence. It’s also provides an opportunity for Jennifer’s attorney to tell the prosecutor and the judge about her progress on the proactive program she started weeks or months ago.

Depending upon the charge, the client’s criminal history and the judge, the case can now go in a number of directions. Here are the different directions:

Option #1 - After an extensive review of the evidence and the options in the case, Jennifer decides she wants to avoid a lengthy prison or jail sentence, and her attorney at this first Pretrial Conference works out a sentencing agreement with the judge. From here, the judge would take Jennifer's plea of guilty or no-contest, and the case would be set for Sentencing in about four to six weeks. The client will be interviewed by probation before Sentencing and Jennifer's final court appearance would be her next appearance.

Option #2 - Progress is made at the first Pretrial Conference, but there are additional issues to sort out, and an adjournment is sought where all parties agree to come back a few weeks later. The next court date will also be called a Pretrial Conference.

Option #3 - Either after one or multiple Pretrial Conferences, a case can be set for a Motion Hearing where the parties will submit motions and briefs to the Court for review of various issues. A common motion to file would be a Motion to Suppress Evidence, where Jennifer's attorney has identified an issue in the case where a good argument can be made that some evidence was illegally seized and the judge could suppress the evidence, which could lead to a dismissal of the entire case.

Sometimes a judge will determine that not only a motion needs to be filed, but testimony needs to be heard by the court with an Evidentiary Hearing. If the case is not dismissed, the matter will proceed to trial for the jury or a jury to decide guilt versus innocence.

Option #4 - Assuming that Jennifer has not resolved her case with Option #1, and she never elected Option #3 or the case was not dismissed after exploring that option, Jennifer is now faced with going to trial on the charges. In Michigan, Jennifer is entitled to a bench or jury trial on the charges. She will either be found guilty or not guilty at trial.

If there is more than one charge, you can be found guilty or not-guilty on some or all of the charges. If found not-guilty on all charges, the case is over; if found guilty on at least one charge, the case will be set for Sentencing where the judge will determine the sentence. For felonies in Michigan, this could be prison, jail, probation, a mix of these or none at all. All felonies in Michigan use the Michigan Legislative Sentencing Guidelines.

Now that we've discussed the Washtenaw Circuit Court, let's now focus on the various district courts across the County.

Chapter Three

Washtenaw County District Courts

The Washtenaw County district courts can be best understood as Ann Arbor and everything else. The 15th District Court in Downtown Ann Arbor handles all cases from the City of Ann Arbor. Everything that is not Ann Arbor is broken down into five additional district courts. Here is a comprehensive breakdown of each district court, the judges, prosecutors, and how a case is handled.

15th District Court - 301 E Huron St, Ann Arbor, MI 48107

The 15th District Court handles all cases from the City of Ann Arbor; if you're charged with a crime or issued a ticket on the campus of the University of Michigan, while tailgating or inside Michigan Stadium, your court case will be handled at this courthouse. The Ann Arbor District Court has three judges and one magistrate, and you could have one of two different prosecutors.

The judges of the 15th District Court are Judge Elizabeth Hines, Judge Karen Valvo and Judge Joseph Burke; the magistrate is Colleen Currie. Each judge is currently assigned a certain category of criminal case with some overlap; the assignments are always changing, but as of the publishing of this book, the current breakdown is the following.

Judge Hines is currently handling all domestic violence and assault cases, with some disorderly conduct, possession of marijuana, minor in possession, fake ID, retail fraud, urinating in public and other non-drunk driving misdemeanors.

Judge Valvo is handling the majority of non-drunk driving cases with the exception of the domestic violence and assault cases. If you're charged with minor in possession, fake ID, disorderly conduct, possession of marijuana, retail fraud, urinating in public and other misdemeanors, it's likely that you will be assigned Judge Valvo. Judge Valvo currently presides over the Veteran's Court and the Mental Health Court.

Judge Burke is currently handling all drunk driving cases, along with presiding over the Ann Arbor Sobriety Court, and does not currently preside over other criminal cases with the rare exception that he is covering another judge's docket.

In addition to their responsibilities at the 15th District Court, all three judges also handle cases at the 14A-1 District Court for the Preliminary Examination/felony cases handled within Washtenaw County.

All three judges do a great job handling their dockets in an efficient and equitable manner. The court is very easy to work with in terms of rescheduling cases and going above and beyond to make sure that each case is handled with the proper care, which the client deserves.

As with the judges, the two prosecutors who handle cases at the 15th District Court are good to work with, and handle cases in a very fair manner for clients who deserve a certain result.

If you're charged with a misdemeanor in Ann Arbor, the prosecutor will either be the Washtenaw County Prosecutor's Office or the City of Ann Arbor. This distinction comes down to the type of offense that you're charged with, your criminal history and the arresting police agency.

As a general rule, if you're arrested or issued a ticket by the Michigan State Police, the University of Michigan Police Department or the Washtenaw County Sheriff's Office, the Washtenaw County Prosecutor's Office will be the prosecutor. If you were arrested or issued a ticket by the Ann Arbor Police Department, your prosecutor will be the City of Ann Arbor.

In addition to the police agency, if you're charged with domestic violence, repeat offense retail fraud, second offense drunk driving and most assault crimes, the Washtenaw County Prosecutor's Office will be the prosecutor. All felonies are handled by Washtenaw County, and not the City of Ann Arbor.

The Ann Arbor District Court is night and day compared with some other courts in Michigan, and if you had to pick a court to have a case, this would probably be the best court in Michigan.

When charged with a crime in Ann Arbor, you may be issued a ticket on the spot with 10-14 days to report to the courthouse, or a report is created and the police officer may tell you that the case will be sent to the prosecutor for review. This review could take a few days, weeks or months, but either way it's time to hire an attorney, and begin a proactive plan from day one. Here are some additional rules of thumb:

#1 - If you're charged with a drunk driving offense, your first court date will be with Judge Burke for an arraignment.

#2- If you're charged with domestic violence, your first court date will be with Judge Hines for an arraignment.

#3 - If you're charged with most other misdemeanors, your case may be assigned to Magistrate Currie who will then send it either Judge Hines or Valvo.

An arraignment is a court date to hear your charges, and enter a plea or guilty or not guilty. If you plead guilty, you then have a criminal record for the crime you have been charged with without any "deal" in place. If you plead not-guilty, then you get a pretrial with one of the judges and one of the prosecutors. The prosecutor is NOT present at the arraignment, and it is simply a waste of time if you can avoid it. Here is how I handle three different types of cases in the Ann Arbor District Court, and the options that could be created for clients.

<u>Case #1 - Possession of Marijuana - University of Michigan Police</u>

I handle a lot of cases that involve a University of Michigan student caught with marijuana in their dorm room while on campus. Most if not all "dorm room" offenses are handled by the University of Michigan Police Department. If the client cooperates, the alleged drugs will be confiscated, and the case will be submitted to the Washtenaw

County Prosecutor's Office, because of the policy agency. This type of case may take a few weeks to be charged, because the drugs must be tested, and the County takes longer than the City to charge cases.

At this time, the client or a family member of the client will reach out to me for information and help with the case. I will explain to them who the prosecutor will be, and who the judge is likely to be assigned the case. More importantly the consequences of a drug conviction.

While providing the details of the charge, I also discuss my proactive program, which will put the client in the best position going forward. This means from day one, we're working on the case outside the courtroom. If you simply sit back and wait to be charged, that in my opinion is the worst decision someone can make; it's wasted time and opportunity. In the next chapter, I will discuss the details of my proactive program, but for now let's assume the client agrees to follow my program, and I accept them as a client.

At this point, I would begin tracking the case, so we're not surprised by charges and an arrest warrant; once charged my team will file my paperwork with the court, prosecutor and the police department. We will begin the information gathering process of obtaining the police reports, witness statements, lab results, and any media (audio or video) created by the police department or from the dorm.

The first court date for this type of case is likely to be with Magistrate Currie, which I will request the court to waive this court date, and give us a court date with the judge. The judge for this type of case is likely to be Judge Valvo, but could be Judge Hines. Once we get the new court date, I will begin discussions with the prosecutor, who in this particular case would be the Washtenaw County Prosecutor's Office.

Once my client and I have reviewed the police reports, we may decide to file motions or set the case for trial if we have discovered viable trial defenses. We will also discuss alternative resolutions, which I may be able to negotiate with the prosecutor and the judge to have the charges dismissed, and kept off of a criminal record. These alternative resolutions are created by my client's proactive efforts outside of the courtroom. It's our goal to create the outcome we want, and have the judge and the prosecutor agree to what we're proposing. Most clients view the prosecutor and judge as the "enemy", but with this sort of charge, it is quite possible to take yourself out of the "punishment column" and into the "education/treatment column" where you can earn a true second chance, and a way to have your case dismissed, but it's really up to how hard you work toward this result.

A possible outcome for this particular case is a dismissal of charges; if that option is not available or offered by the prosecutor and judge, then a trial may be the best option, but only if it is in the best interest of the client.

<u>Case #2 - Drunk Driving Charges - City of Ann Arbor PD</u>

When a client contacts me about a DUI charge in Ann Arbor, the first two questions are usually "what police department arrested you?" and "do you have any prior offenses?"

These are important questions, because it will determine who the prosecutor will be on the case. In our example, the arresting police agency is the City of Ann Arbor Police Department, so it will be the City of Ann Arbor Prosecutor unless the client has any prior offenses.

At the 15th District Court, all DUI cases are handled by Judge Burke, and we skip Magistrate Currie, because Judge Burke sets the bond conditions, and does not want a lapse in time without specialized testing and monitoring in place. I agree with how this is handled, because Judge Burke is the DUI judge, and should handle the case from A to Z.

Depending upon what your blood alcohol level is, Judge Burke may or may not have you test daily for alcohol, and randomly for drugs. Regardless of what the court is going to do, I typically have all of my clients alcohol testing from day one along with other elements of my proactive program, which I will discuss in the next chapter.

When a client contacts me for help with their Ann Arbor DUI case, I explain the process from beginning to end, and have them review my proactive program, which is geared toward what we can expect from Judge Burke, and the prosecutor. If the client is willing to follow my proactive program then we get to work immediately.

I will file my paperwork with the court, prosecutor and the police department, and I will request that the arraignment be combined with a pretrial. This allows the client to handle both the arraignment and the pretrial in one court date, and gives us additional time to obtain the police reports, test results, video, audio and other evidence in the case.

For a DUI case in Ann Arbor there are two distinct directions to go, and my clients go down both paths until we determine the best route depending upon the goals of the client and the strengths and weaknesses of the case.

The case may be set for motions, or be set for a bench or jury trial. If we can accomplish the client's goals for having the charges dismissed or reduced then we may explore negotiation with the judge and prosecutor, and use our proactive efforts to clear the way for the outcome we want. It's important to create multiple options, and make a pros and cons list for each option. My clients create leverage with the information gathering stage, and demonstrate real action, rather than mere words on the proactive program.

Case #3 - Open Intoxicant - Ann Arbor Police Department

I handle a lot of these types of cases during football season due to the high volume of drinking before, during or after Michigan Football games. Out of towners are typically the targets of the police department, and are totally unaware that drinking on the sidewalk could lead to a misdemeanor crime.

I receive calls all day and night from people who need my help to avoid a criminal record, and I will discuss this criminal offense in greater detail later in this book, but for now, let's discuss how we handle this case at the 15th District Court.

Once the client hires me, I file my paperwork with the court, prosecutor and the police department. Typically the only paperwork on this case is the ticket from the police department, which the client already has in their possession, but sometimes, the officer generates a police report, and their may be video and audio of the incident.

This type of case is set for a court date within 10-14 days of when it happened, but many of my clients are not from the area, and worry about taking a day off from work to attend court with no idea what to do about their criminal case. Fortunately for my clients, my paperwork will cancel this need to appear within that period of time, and our case is assigned to a judge, which is typically Judge Valvo. The prosecutor in this case will be the City of Ann Arbor.

If the client is from out of town or cannot take off from work or delegate their responsibilities to somebody else for the day, I can typically gain permission to have my client excused from attending court, and can resolve the case in a favorable manner.

To recap, each case at the 15th District Court begins with a police agency, which then submits the case to the prosecutor, which then brings the case to the courthouse to begin with either the magistrate of one of the three judges. Each judge handles a certain type of case, and the prosecutor is determined by a number of factors. No matter the judge, charge or prosecutor, it's important to hire an attorney from day one who can help you navigate the process, put you on a proactive plan from day one, and create options for resolving your case.

14A-1 District Court - 4133 Washtenaw Ave Ann Arbor, MI

The 14A-1 District Court is typically referred to as the service center or the Pittsfield Township Court. This particular court handles all felony matters prior to the heading to the 22nd Circuit Court. Information about that process can be found earlier in this book, for now we're only going to focus on how the court handles misdemeanors.

The Pittsfield Township District Court presides over Pittsfield Township, Augusta Township, Superior Township, the Village of Barton Hills and the City of Ypsilanti. Judge Richard E. Conlin currently presides over all the misdemeanors at the 14A-1 Court, and the prosecutor is typically the Washtenaw County Prosecutor's Office or the Pittsfield Township Prosecutor. There are other prosecutors, but only a small handful of cases are handled by these officials.

Like other courts in Washtenaw County, the arresting police agency will usually determine who the prosecutor is going to be. The most common police agencies with this court are the Washtenaw County Sheriff's Office, Michigan State Police and Pittsfield Township Police Department. The three most common offenses I see in this court are drunk driving, retail fraud and possession of marijuana.

This court is really good about scheduling and moving things around, along with granting permission to travel during your case. This is one of the few courts in Michigan where it truly feels like a client is innocent until proven guilty. Judge Conlin treats clients with a lot of respect, and clients come away with a good feeling about the process. Both prosecutors are good to work with, and handle cases in an equitable manner. Here are two examples of how cases are handled at the 14A-1 District Court:

<u>Case #1 - Retail Fraud Third Degree - Pittsfield Township PD</u>

If the client is a first offender and the arresting police agency is Pittsfield Township, we will be working with the Pittsfield Township Prosecutor. The Pittsfield Prosecutor is currently a law firm which is hired by the Township to prosecute cases. This means that the attorneys who handle the prosecution are also private attorneys with their own clients. In my experience, this is quite favorable for my clients who follow my proactive program (more on this later). When a prosecutor can reflect on their own clients when considering my client's circumstance, we're usually able to have more success in obtaining a desired result.

For this particular case, I would discuss the process from beginning to end with the client, and tell them more about my proactive program. If my client agrees to follow my program, I would file my attorney paperwork with the Pittsfield Township Police Department, the Pittsfield Prosecutor and with Judge Conlin's staff at the courthouse. This process would allow us access to the police reports, video and other evidence, and allow me to begin discussions with the prosecutor. It will also allow us to control scheduling matters when it comes to the arraignment process and setting future court dates.

For a retail fraud case in Pittsfield Township, we want a pretrial where the prosecuting attorney is present, so we can work toward a possible dismissal of charges. Judge Conlin is very accommodating, and will usually do same-day sentencing, which saves my client additional trips to the courthouse, and lets the client get probation over with sooner than if they had to wait an additional 4-6 weeks for sentencing.

When a client contacts me about this sort of case, I ask which police department arrested them or issued a ticket, what store they were in, and if they have any prior record. Based on those answers, we can learn a lot about the case, and begin the process of setting goals, and reaching those goals by being proactive from day one.

<u>Case #2 - Drunk Driving - Washtenaw County Sheriff's Department</u>

If a client is arrested for a DUI in the Pittsfield Township area, they will automatically have the Washtenaw County Prosecutor's Office on their case if it's a second offense. If it's a first offense, but the police agency is the Sheriff's Department, Michigan State Police or occasionally the University of Michigan Police Department, the prosecutor will also be the County.

When charged with a DUI offense at the 14A-1 Court, my client and I will discuss my proactive program in order to best position our case with the prosecutor and Judge Conlin. My attorney appearance will combine the arraignment and the pretrial, allowing us to combine two court dates into one, and give us time to obtain the evidence in the case.

In my experience, cases handled by Judge Conlin are typically probation cases, meaning jail is a rare outcome unless there are some unusual circumstances. In my experience, the County prosecutor is less likely to dismiss or reduce charges compared to a case handled by Pittsfield Township, but even the Township can be quite strict with certain cases. My client and I are usually able to create the option of a reduction in charges if they follow my proactive program, but if the facts lend themselves to defenses at trial, my client may elect to test the evidence with a bench or jury trial.

14A-2 District Court - 415 W. Michigan Ave Ypsilanti, MI 48197

The 14A-2 District Court in Washtenaw County handles misdemeanor cases for the City of Ypsilanti, including Eastern Michigan University as well as, Ann Arbor Township, Augusta Township, Salem Township, Superior Township and the Village of Barton Hills.

The most common police department's handling cases for this particular court are the Washtenaw County Sheriff's Office, Ypsilanti Police Department, Michigan State Police and the Eastern Michigan Police Department. The majority of cases in this court are handled by the Washtenaw County Prosecutor's Office and the City of Ypsilanti Prosecutor.

Like other courts, the arresting agency will usually determine who the prosecutor is: Washtenaw County Sheriff's Office (State Prosecutor) vs City of Ypsilanti Police Department (City Prosecutor). The Judge who will handle the case as of the publishing of this book is Judge Kirk W. Tabbey who is a very reasonable and fair judge.

The most common offenses that I handle from this particular court are drunk driving cases within the jurisdiction of the court, and underage drinking and possession of marijuana cases stemming from the Eastern Michigan University campus.

The 14A-2 District Court and Judge Tabbey have shown tremendous support for a proactive approach in the past. Depending upon who the prosecutor is on the case, it is quite possible to get substantial reductions on drunk driving offenses, and very favorable sentences. I have had clients in the past accomplish so much proactively that Judge Tabbey did not give my client any jail or probation, and my client saved their driver's license.

It is also quite possible to work out dismissals on MIP and possession of marijuana charges with the prosecutor and the judge if the client is able to accomplish the proactive goals set for their case. The 14A-2 Court is a very favorable court to handle a criminal case.

14A-3 District Court - 122 S. Main St Chelsea, MI 48118

This particular Washtenaw County court handles all misdemeanors from the City of Chelsea, the Village of Dexter and the Townships of Dexter, Lima, Lyndon, Northfield, Scio, Sylvan and Webster.

The Washtenaw County Prosecutor's Office handles the majority of the cases at the 14A-3 District Court, and Judge Conlin is the assigned judge out in Chelsea. The Chelsea District Court is a very fair court, and like the Pittsfield cases, handles cases in a manner which echoes innocent until proven guilty, as bond conditions are set, but not an early punishment in disguise.

This Court is accommodating with travel requests, and re-scheduling court dates if necessary. Clients leave the Chelsea District Court feeling that their case was handled in a respectable manner, and always tell me how much they enjoyed Judge Conlin, and his staff.

Some cases are more difficult than others when it comes to plea-bargaining, because the Washtenaw County Prosecutor's Office handles the majority of cases at this Court. This means it is even more important for my clients to be proactive from day one, because we need to show exceptional progress and results in order to receive an exceptional outcome. I tend to handle a lot of drunk driving cases, along with some domestic violence, retail fraud and illegal possession of marijuana and alcohol at the Chelsea District Court.

The Washtenaw County Sheriff's Office and the Michigan State Police make most of the arrests in this area, and a good portion of the offenses involve a car or truck. If you have CDL or a CPL that is an important thing to tell your attorney when you first speak to them about your case.

I've found the probation department at the 14A-3 District Court to be easy to work with, and they are willing to work with clients with special requests such as a travel and relocation requests. While they are good to work with, the client needs to show them compliance and a willingness to follow all instructions and rules.

If you've been charged with a crime with a court date at the 14A-3 District Court in Chelsea, we will discuss the process from beginning to end, and how the proactive program will put you in a strong position to create options in your case.

We will want to set the case for a dual arraignment and pretrial in order to avoid missing a day of work to simply have your case rescheduled. This also allows us to buy additional time to obtain the evidence in the case, and put in additional time on the proactive program, which I will discuss in the next chapter.

<u>14A-4 District Court - 1000 N. Maple Rd Saline, MI 48176</u>

The 14A-4 District Court handles all misdemeanor cases for the Cities of Saline and Milan, the Townships of Bridgewater, Freedom, Lodi, Manchester, Saline, Sharon and York, as well as the Village of Manchester. The assigned judge as of the publishing of this book is Judge Cedric Simpson.

The Saline District Court handles a lot of drunk driving cases, other traffic misdemeanors, retail fraud, possession of marijuana, underage drinking and property offenses.

The most common police departments that submit cases to this court are the Michigan State Police, the Washtenaw County Sheriff's Department and the Saline Police Department. The Washtenaw County Prosecutor's Office is typically the prosecutor on most cases, but I tend to handle a lot of DUI and other driving cases with the City/Township prosecuting attorneys.

My experience handling cases in this court is very positive, because all of the prosecutors are very amenable to my clients proactive measures, and Judge Simpson is a judge who is willing to view a client on their full resume rather than the single case before him. He regularly gives clients the opportunity to earn back the trust of the Court and the community, and gives people a second chance.

When a client hires me for a Saline District Court case, we discuss exactly what Judge Simpson is looking for from a client, and discuss the different prosecutors who could be on the case. The Saline District Court tends to set tougher bond conditions than some other courts in the area, but this doesn't matter, because my clients are already testing for drugs and alcohol before stepping foot in a courtroom. The Saline District Court tends to schedule sentencing further out than most courts in the County, so my clients seek immediate sentencing if possible in order to expedite the process.

14-B District Court - 7200 S. Huron River Dr. Ypsilanti, MI 48197

The 14-B District Court is sometimes the forgotten Washtenaw County District Court, because it's not Ann Arbor, and it's not part of the 14A District Courts (Pittsfield, Ypsilanti, Chelsea and Saline). It is also confused with the 14A-2 Court, because most people don't realize the difference between the courts.

The 14-B District Court is limited to misdemeanor cases arising out of Ypsilanti Township whereas the 14A-2 District Court handles City of Ypsilanti cases. The 14-B court handles a lot of drug possession cases, along with drunk driving cases, and there are two different prosecutors.

The Washtenaw County Prosecutor's Office handles all cases originating from the Washtenaw County Sheriff's Department, Michigan State Police, and all second offense drunk driving cases, along with some other limited cases. All other cases are handled by the Ypsilanti Township Prosecutor.

If you're charged with a crime at the 14-B District Court, your file may be assigned to Magistrate Mark Nelson who handles a lot of cases early in the process, but the judge on all cases is Judge Charles Pope. Both Magistrate Nelson and Judge Pope are fair and equitable, and are very reasonable when it comes to travel requests, bond conditions and sentencing.

In my experience working with clients at the 14-B District Court, there is a tremendous opportunity for a client to shine on a proactive program. I would find it quite surprising for anyone else other than my own clients to be following a proactive plan at this particular court house. When my client walks into court having already accomplished 4-5 different proactive measures, such as community service, alcohol education classes, successfully passed proactive drug screens and other measures, and they are compared to the other thirty-five defendants sitting in court, my client looks like a rockstar, who will stand-out, and likely receive a better result than the average defendant on that given day.

CHAPTER FOUR

WINNING- "A PROACTIVE APPROACH TO YOUR CASE"

When you're charged with a crime in Washtenaw County, potential clients always tell me how scared they are, or just how nervous they are about going to court. I explain to them that they are likely scared or nervous about things that are statistically unlikely to even happen. We discuss each thing that is making them feel that way, and we can usually take at least of them off of the table.

I tell them that it may feel like nerves or terror, but it's really about what I call "the great unknown". A person who has never been charged with a crime is completely in the dark about the process, and likely doesn't even know where the courthouse is located. A person who has been charged in the past, is equally anxious, because it may be a different type of charge, or they are returning to court with a record now, which they are worried will eliminate many of their options they had the first time they appeared in court.

Once we better understand that the client is more anxious than anything, we begin to understand why they are feeling like that. The client is anxious because they have a job, a family, goals in life, and having a criminal record, losing a license, going to jail, and other consequences will simply change their life, sometimes in dramatic ways. All of those feelings are valid, because a criminal charge is the first step to major changes in someone's life.

The client feels the weight of these consequences closing in around them at a rapid pace, and they don't know how to react. Clients feel powerless against the "other side", which they believe to be the judge, the prosecutor, the police, probation and society. Fear of what others will think begins to set in, and a lot of clients at this point simply throw their hands up in the air, and give up, or try to get it over with as soon as possible.

The worst, but most natural thing to do, is think about giving up, and simply accept the outcome for what it is, because what power does the client have to change it?

Many clients first instinct, is "well, maybe if a call a lawyer, he/she will know how to help". Yes, hiring a lawyer is a good first step, because according to the State Bar of Michigan, that particular lawyer is deemed to have the training to assist clients with their legal needs. The problem that I see with the process, is that clients believe that all lawyers are created equal, and it's like buying a flat-screen television.

For a television, you look online, visit stores and simply make your decision based upon it being a flat-screen, and the price they are offered; most people compare by price, and just make a quick decision, because they all seem relatively the same.

ALL LAWYERS ARE NOT THE SAME. Any lawyer can put on a suit, walk into court with you, use big words and tell you that you got a great result. Will did you? Were you treated like everyone else in court, because that's how you feel about yourself? Did the process feel like an assembly line where you were simply handed off without actually doing anything to make your case different from anyone else? What if you could put in the hard work upfront, and earn something better?

If you're looking to buy or build a house with a roof, walls and doors, then you can hire any licensed crew to assemble a roof, walls and doors, just like you can hire one of thousands of licensed lawyers in Michigan, and get a similar quality. If you're looking to build something that is a reflection of who you have been in the past, present and the future then you want to hire a builder that can match your vision and customize the outcome of the house. This is the same exact thing that is possible in a courtroom. People just don't realize the possibilities until they encounter it.

If you're charged with a crime in Washtenaw County, I strongly encourage you to do something other than HIRE A LAWYER. That is the easiest thing to do, and quite frankly the laziest thing you can do other than skip your court date. If you want to take your case seriously, you should be RESEARCHING LAWYERS, and that doesn't mean comparing prices and what the lawyer says the outcome will be.

It's unethical, and misleading to tell a client what the result of a case will be until, the lawyer has fully examined the facts of the case, identified and spoken with the prosecutor and judge, and discussed in detail your criminal past, and your goals for the case.

There are two things you should do when charged with a crime in Washtenaw County. Set goals, and have a plan to reach those goals. Hiring an attorney can be part of that process, but paying a lawyer doesn't create goals or a plan. Just like paying a construction crew doesn't provide a custom blueprint to build your home. If you let a lawyer or a construction crew simply "handle" your case, you're bound to get the same result as everyone else in court that day, and to get a cookie cutter home that matches what all the neighbors have.

When a potential client contacts me, the first thing I do is call a timeout. The potential client is asking me how much I charge, and what's going to happen to them. Good questions, but not the most productive questions to begin the process. I tell them to put those questions aside for now, and ask the following questions:

- How old are you?
- Have you ever been in trouble before?
- Where did this happen?
- What happened?
- What police department was involved?
- Do you know the charges?
- Do you have a court date set yet?

Depending upon the facts, I will go into more detail, but the key is to simply learn more about the case, before I can answer the original questions of how much I charge, and what's going to happen.

Before i even get to those questions, I tell my client about my exclusive representation policy, and how all of my clients are required to be on my proactive program from day one. I do not take cases where the client is not willing, or even unsure about participating. I have too many potential clients that are motivated to follow my program, to waste my time with a client who is not as motivated as I am.

Based on my experience as a prosecutor in New York City, and here in Michigan, I've worked on the other side of thousands of cases against other criminal attorneys. Over the year, I identified what worked, and didn't work with their clients, and took that experience into private practice, and developed a comprehensive program, which my clients now follow from day one.

The philosophy of my approach is simply WINNING. Most people viewing WINNING as a victory at trial or getting a case dismissed; those results would certainly qualify as WINNING, but the process is not that black and white, and those results are quite rare. In my experience, there are a number of ways to WIN your case, and each stage of the case can go a number of different ways.

WINNING comes down to opportunity, and time is a valuable asset in a criminal case. With that time, you need a plan. With that plan, you set goals within the framework of the facts of your case. By setting those goals, and laying out a comprehensive plan, you're committed to reaching those goals, and creating a customized outcome. An outcome that may not have been available to you without your plan.

It's an opportunity to not be judged solely on your present case, but instead on your past, present and where you're going in the future. Right now, the judge, prosecutor, police, probation and your community are simply looking at the police report, the charges and the likely default outcome of this case, and allowing the case to define who you will be going forward.

That's simply not fair to be judged on a single moment in time. It gives no credit to past accomplishments, present responsibilities and future goals. And I don't mean your lawyer telling the prosecutor that you have a job or kids to take care of; words have very little value in court.

WINNING in Washtenaw County is about actions, because you allegedly committed this crime(s) with all of this already in place, and it didn't prevent you from being charged with the present offense. If your family, job and responsibilities could be impacted by your DUI charge, you should not have put them in jeopardy to begin with, so those words alone don't mean anything to a prosecutor and judge.

It's more about what you've done in reaction to the charges, and projecting what you will do in the future. I will get into more detail on how you can WIN your DUI case a moment.

To quote a local judge "if you wanted that to happen, you would have already been doing it before coming here to court". That's what being proactive is all about. Committing yourself to learning from the situation you've been put in. Being charged with a crime in Washtenaw County throws you into a deep hole; any lawyer can tell you to climb out; but that isn't very helpful. What's the plan to get out?

Even if your case is ultimately dismissed or you're found not guilty, being in this situation is an opportunity to learn more about yourself and your decisions going forward. You may be a great person, mom, dad, husband, wife, employer, business owner or productive member of your community, but you still found yourself in this bad situation. A police officer found enough reason to arrest you, a prosecutor found enough to charge you, what are you going to do now to help yourself?

I only agree to take on those clients that are willing to be proactive, because it's my role as your attorney, to not only help you inside the courtroom, but help you outside the courtroom. You were charged with a crime for some reason, we are going to explore why, and help you learn from it, and set goals for going to court. Each type of case has it's own elements that we make part of the plan, but each plan is customized to the individual client's needs and specific facts of their case.

Let's now explore the different plans, which I put into play for clients on a few different types of cases. I will give what I believe is the judge's point of view on each case, what the prosecutor is thinking, and how we overcome the perceptions of your case from day one.

Winning "A Proactive Approach to Retail Fraud"

Judge's Take: For retail fraud cases in Washtenaw County, the majority, if not all of the judges will view a first offender as someone who simply used poor judgment. If there is a history of theft crimes then a judge begins to wonder just how many times this person got away with stealing other than the current case. First offenders get more of the benefit of the doubt, but again, has this person stolen items before, but simply was not caught?

A judge in Washtenaw County will also look at the store, the items and the value of those items when passing judgment on your case. If you're young and stealing clothing or makeup then it's likely you've done it before in their eyes, and you are likely to do it again. If you're a bit older with no record, and you're taking food at Meijer, a judge may look at the case and think there must be something going on with this person, unless it was a misunderstanding of sorts.

No matter your record or age, a judge in Washtenaw County will wonder if this arrest, charge and appearing in court is enough to send a message that this is not acceptable behavior. They have no way of judging if that message is clear, or if this is going in one ear, and out the other, and you're likely to do this again in the future. A judge doesn't know if you're a good person in a bad situation or a bad person in one of many bad situations.

Prosecutor's Take: All prosecutors in Washtenaw County are pretty much on board with whatever a judge and defense lawyer are working on. If the client is a first offender, and eligible for some sort of dismissal, the prosecutor will usually support this plan. As a former prosecutor in New York and Michigan, I typically viewed a shoplifting case as someone simply acting foolish or trying to get away with something; from working with clients every day on these cases, I now understand there is a lot more behind these crimes, but prosecutors aren't that educated on the mindset of the client.

As long as my client can show the prosecutor that they are motivated to make some positive changes in their life and learn from the incident, they will go along with our plan. This applies to the Washtenaw County Prosecutor's Office and all of the city and township prosecutors. It's important to maintain a proactive plan from the beginning to the end of your case, and not to stop once the prosecutor has agreed to dismiss your case.

Being Proactive: I approach every retail fraud case with the goal of showing the judge and prosecutor that this was an isolated moment in time, and my client is a good person who simply made a bad choice.

If my client has a history of retail fraud then we approach it in a manner, which the client can greatly benefit from education and treatment, and has lacked this approach in the past.

The first thing we do is proactive community service; generally 20-40 hours is required, and the non-profit should be located in Washtenaw County. If the client does not live in the area, I sometimes tell the client that volunteer work outside the area is acceptable, but the preference is to do the volunteer work inside the community. By doing volunteer work, it's a clear example of the real you, and how you have a positive influence in the community, and you're not simply a thief.

A retail fraud crime on your record means a crime of theft, dishonesty and fraud, which will eliminate you from almost every job. Because of your choice, the store, the police, the prosecutor, the judge and an entire courthouse is now working on your case. By doing community service work, you're self-imposing a punishment, which is likely to keep you out of jail, and will hopefully eliminate the need to do any additional volunteer work at a later time.

It's a currency to exchange with the judge and prosecutor that you're willing to take hours out of your life to improve your community and not commit crimes.

Next we explore treatment and education. All of my clients do a retail fraud educational class, which is usually 4 to 8 hours in length, which helps them explore why this happened, and how going forward this can be avoided. Along with the treatment and education, my clients attend support group meetings to talk about their case with others charged with similar offenses.

These retail fraud meetings are like an AA for alcoholics, but the purpose is more educational, and to be an impact experience. If from attending the meetings, you realize the problem is greater than you thought, we adjust and add additional elements.

At this meetings, clients encounter people from different backgrounds, ages, genders, professions, education levels and financial means. It helps the client cope with their case, and understand that they are not alone in facing the charge, and can learn from others who have been charged with the offense more than once, or have lost jobs, gone to jail and had their life ruined because of this offense.

It's a great tool along with the educational class to show the prosecutor and judge that you're feeling the full impact of being charged with the offense, and the message has been received, and you're learning from it.

If a judge and prosecutor believe you've learned your lesson, they are likely to agree to some sort of dismissal, but if they don't think the message has gotten across then a judge may consider jail, and a prosecutor may not dismiss your case. Why should someone who clearly hasn't learned anything from their case be allowed to go forward in life without this on their record; shouldn't others be on notice not to trust this person? The client controls how their case is perceived, and being proactive is the best way to control that perception.

Winning "A Proactive Approach to Drug Possession Crimes"

Judge's Take: Washtenaw County is a system which strongly supports rehabilitation, treatment and second chances for individuals charged with drug offenses. This is great for clients who actually have a drug addiction, because the judges will allow clients to seek treatment rather than jail, but what if you don't have an addiction, but you simply possessed drugs for recreational purposes?

How do judges view these clients? If it's marijuana, some of the judges acknowledge that this substance might be legal some day, but for now it is against the law, and will treat the case accordingly. The number one thing on the judge's mind is not using or possessing that drug during the case. Most if not all the judges in Washtenaw County will order random or scheduled drug testing during the case, and if you're placed on probation, you will be tested during the duration of probation. If you test positive while on bond or probation, you could be sent to jail or lose any first offender type outcomes, which you previously earned.

Judges in Washtenaw County will support dismissal outcomes for possession cases if the client has demonstrated that they are no longer using the drug, and are not likely to use it illegally in the future. Judges realize that a drug charge on a resume and criminal record will be a complete disaster for employment and education. A client can be denied student loans because of a drug conviction.

A judge will look at what you have done since the incident to see if you're heading in the right path since the offense, or if you've simply sat back and waited to come to court.

Prosecutor's Take: The prosecutors in Washtenaw County view drugs in a similar way as the judges. Generally speaking, the prosecutors in the County will support treatment over punishment, but they charged you with a crime offense for a reason, because you broke the law. A prosecutor may not be as easy to convince to support a dismissal of charges, and the client needs to really demonstrate that the offense is isolated, and not likely to happen again. How have you reacted to being charged with a drug possession case?

When a prosecutor charges a case, they do so because someone broke the law, and by charging the offense, they hope that it will act as a deterrent for future offenses; both the person charged, and others who see people getting charged, and want to avoid that same fate. If cases are being dismissed, does that really accomplish the goal of the prosecutor?

When I was a prosecutor in New York and Michigan, I viewed drug possession crimes as black and white. This is not an offense where there is a misunderstanding of sorts; if someone has an illegal drug on them, they are intentionally doing something that they know is illegal, and they could also be selling it, and harming other people.

From representing clients in private practice, I have a slightly different view of the offense. Most people who possess drugs in Michigan, are not doing so for evil purposes, or bad people. The client simply enjoys using the drug, just like someone enjoys alcohol, and they are willing to risk getting in trouble with the law to continue using the drug.

If it's a marijuana offense, I tell my client to obtain a medical marijuana card once their case is over if they really want to use the drug. If the client is possessing a controlled substance narcotic, I remind them that going forward without a valid prescription they are risking everything to give up their habit and pleasure they get from using the drug. I provide them exactly how the prosecutor views their case, because I used to be in that position for many years.

Being Proactive: The first thing I do for any client charged with a drug offense in Washtenaw County is tell the client to immediately stop using the drug. We discuss their last usage, and when the substance will be out of their system; at the very least the plan is to show their levels are going down. We discuss taking drugs tests during the case even if we're not ordered by the judge, because we can't walk into court and tell a prosecutor and judge that the client is no longer using the drug without proof of it. Without the test, only the client knows the truth, and the client is the one charged with breaking the law, and has low credibility.

By demonstrating that the client is no longer using the drug, it is easier to convince a prosecutor and judge that the client is not likely to repeat the offense, and will not be an issue moving forward. On top of the testing, we add in an educational component to provide further tools for the client to learn more about the negative impact of drug use, and avoiding further charges with the court.

One big thing clients learn from the educational portion is about "drugged drinking"; any level of marijuana or another controlled substance in the client's blood can be considered the same as drunk driving. Many clients use drugs for years, and drive without realizing that this is no different than being over the legal limit with alcohol.

Depending on the level of charges, a lot of my clients undergo a substance abuse screening and assessment by a licensed professional in order to further explore any pending issues. If the professional recommended treatment or classes, I tell my client to follow this recommendation. There is nothing better than proactively seeking out help from a professional, being recommended to follow a course of treatment, and complete this recommendation during the case. A judge and prosecutor are going to be extremely impressed, and if you've started or completed the recommendation, a judge may not sentence you any further than what you have completed.

All of my clients also add in community service hours for the reasons stated earlier in this chapter. It's simply another positive tool to show a prosecutor and judge that the client has earned the right to have a second chance, and potentially avoid a drug conviction on their record.

Winning "A Proactive Approach to Drunk Driving"

Judge's Take: Over the years, the offense of drunk driving has earned a very negative stigma in media coverage. A DUI is no longer a slap on the wrist crime, as judges are feeling pressure from the media, advocacy groups and other government entities to punish drunk drivers as a deterrent for future offenses. Some judges in Michigan have really taken this to heart, and send first offenders to jail on every single case no matter the circumstances.

Fortunately for clients charged in Washtenaw County, there is no current judge who has a firm policy of sending first offenders to jail. There are judges who will send a first offender to jail if it is warranted, but it is not a regular practice. Just because someone doesn't receive jail on a first offense, doesn't mean that the judges aren't taking major action in other ways. People charged with drunk driving in Washtenaw County can receive two years of probation with daily alcohol testing, and a host of intensive treatment programs and weeks worth of community service. Driver's licenses are lost and people lose jobs because of it .

If someone is charged with a second offense DUI in Washtenaw County, the law states that the offender must go to jail for a minimum of 5 days with at least 48 hours served in a row. Judges in the County have different views on this wording, and some follow it closer than others. Some judges in Washtenaw County send people to jail for longer periods of time, and some find ways around it. One alternative to jail in Washtenaw County for a DUI is Sobriety Court or the Mental Health Court.

The question of jail is only a small part of how a judge views a DUI case in Washtenaw County. Testing for alcohol during the case varies by judge and court house, and different probation departments treat testing in different ways. No judge in Washtenaw County wants someone drinking while on bond or probation, but each judge approaches this issue in a different manner.

The judges in Washtenaw County overall are willing to give the client the benefit of the doubt with a first offense misdemeanor. I wouldn't say the County as a whole is any tougher on DUI offenses than other counties in the area. If you go out to Oakland County and some areas of Wayne County, you'll run into much more difficult judges.

Judges in Washtenaw County want to send the right message about DUI cases, but also allow the client charged to learn from the incident, and make better choices going forward. Washtenaw County is the ideal landscape for a proactive program to have a major impact on the direction of my client's case. Being proactive from day one can lead to reduction or dismissal of charges, avoiding jail, better bond conditions, saving a driver's license, and a lighter overall sentence.

<u>Prosecutor's Take:</u> The prosecutors in Washtenaw County are pretty strict when it comes to drunk driving charges. They will offer reductions in cases when warranted, but will not reduce to anything below a drunk driving offense. Some prosecutors in the County will not reduce a case at all if there are certain facts or circumstances.

Typically the Washtenaw County Prosecutor's Office will listen to the reasons why a dismissal or reduction should be granted, but they are looking for a very compelling and unique reason, which most clients cannot provide without a proactive plan in place. If the circumstances are present to warrant such a result, the client must back it up with real actions outside the courtroom. It can be the difference between losing and keeping your driver's license, and having a DUI conviction on your record.

In my experience, most of the city and township prosecutors in Washtenaw County are a bit more open to reductions and dismissals, but are also looking for a compelling reason to do so. The way a prosecutor views a drunk driving case is more perception based than any other misdemeanor offense; prosecutors handle DUI cases more seriously than some felonies. The last thing a prosecutor wants to happen, is to cut a deal with a client then have that client turn around and hurt or kill someone as a drunk driver in the future; the media and the community are going to look at that prosecutor as being at fault if the client got off lightly the first go around.

If the client is charged with a second or third offense (felony), the Washtenaw County Prosecutor's Office does not even consider a reduction in charges. And even if they did, it would not change the Secretary of State penalties of loss of license for an extended period of time and immobilization of your vehicle.

Prosecutors are looking for justification and a compelling reasons to do something special on a drunk driving case. They need something to rely on to show why they did what they did, which is why I target my proactive program directly as this mindset.

<u>Being Proactive:</u> When I work with a client charged with drunk driving in Washtenaw County, we need to place a bookmark on the date of the incident and establish a clear before and after. Whatever has happened in the past was clearly not enough to avoid the decision my client made to get behind a wheel; the client may not be guilty at all, but an officer saw enough to submit the case to the prosecution who agreed, and went ahead with charges. While we discuss what my client has accomplished in the past, it is better to focus on the present and the future.

The 800 pound elephant in the room with a DUI case is a pattern of drunk driving being present. Most people charged with a DUI are not drunk driving for the first time; all prosecutors and judges assume this is only the first time they've been caught, and if the client is charged with a second of third offense, this strengthens that assumption. My client and I understand this perception, and plan for it with a number of proactive measures.

I require all of my clients charged with a DUI offense in Washtenaw County to undergo a substance abuse screening and assessment before we even go to court. I am not an expert in the substance abuse field, and neither is my client. Most people with alcohol issues don't know it, or will not admit to it. My client cannot go in front of a judge, and I can't speak on my client's behalf and say my client doesn't have an alcohol problem, because we have no idea if they do or not. Simply never having been charged with a DUI, does not mean the client does not have an alcohol problem. There are millions of problem drinkers in the world who have not been charged with a DUI.

The best thing my client can do, is get screened and assessed, and the results to be that they do not have an alcohol problem, which will go a long way in resolving their case in a favorable way. If the results come back that my client has a moderate or severe issue, we've now created a great opportunity to show the prosecutor and judge why this happened, and proactively address it before being ordered to do so. We turn a perceived negative into a positive just like we do with everything else.

Along with screening and following all recommendations, my clients attend AA meetings in order to better understand their own case, and lingering issues. My client may not have an alcohol problem, but they can hear from others that might, and compare themselves. The most important part of going to AA is the impact experience. A client hearing the stories of other people who have lost jobs, family members, been divorced, became sick, and other negative results due to alcohol can really open up their eyes even further about the impact of alcohol.

In my view it is not enough for a client to see their case in a vacuum, because, it's likely that my client was not hurt, and nobody else was involved or injured. It's likely my client will be able to keep his/her license, and move on from the case with little long-term impact. While that is our goal, and most of my clients follow that path, does it really provide a long-term solution?

I want my clients to experience the very worst of what their case could have been, because judges and prosecutors think that way. Just because you didn't hurt or kill yourself, or another person, doesn't mean your actions are any better than the person who is charged with a more serious crime for killing someone. It really comes down to luck; it's like playing Russian Roulette; when you drink and drive, you're spinning the barrel when it comes to someone being injured or killed.

In 2014, there were 71,378 injuries due to traffic incidents and 876 deaths in Michigan; that's a lot of people impacted by driver's, now add alcohol, and things get a lot worse. If my client feels the full impact of what could have happened, and we can demonstrate this to a judge and prosecutor, now, not only will we get a better result in court, but you're never going to put yourself in this situation again, and you're going to make sure other don't who may find themselves in the same situation.

In the end, nobody likes drunk driving; even clients charged with a DUI are really ashamed of what happened, and want to make sure it doesn't happen again. It is easy to say, but more difficult to accomplish. I only work with clients who are willing to work hard to make sure they have the tools in place to make better decisions going forward.

There is no sure way to avoid a DUI from happening again, because it's easy to drive a car, and it's easy to drink alcohol; nobody plans to combine the two, but it happens nearly 40,000 times a year in Michigan, and that's only a small fraction, because not everyone is caught in the act.

Along with the above measures, I have my clients take additional alcohol awareness classes, enter treatment and counseling, and test for alcohol and drugs. In Washtenaw County, some judges do not test for alcohol while on bond, and while that is generally viewed as a good thing, I would rather be able to confidently tell a judge my client has not had a drink or used illegal drugs since the incident. Because my client has been testing twice a day for alcohol, and my client has not used illegal drugs (we have a negative ten-panel drug screen in court with us), we can back up these statements. If a client is not willing to make that commitment then I cannot represent them.

If a client is truly serious about getting the best result inside and outside the courtroom, they will use the downtime during their case to show the prosecutor, judge, police, and the community how they reacted to being charged with a DUI. If you're guilty, innocent or you can't remember what happened, you can greatly benefit from this opportunity in life. Hundreds of potential clients contact me each year with DUI charges, and I turn down a good number of cases because clients simply just want their cases dropped or reduced. They are not interested in actually discussing how you get to that result, and they are not interested in making changes in their life; I can almost guarantee those clients will not be satisfied with the result they receive in court, and will not learn a thing from the case, and likely be the client who contacts me again in a year with a second DUI offense.

I am very confident that based on my experience as a prosecutor and as an attorney who practices daily in Washtenaw County, that if handled in a proactive manner from day one, a client can not only avoid jail, keep their license, and severely limit their sentence for their DUI charge, but also avoid future drunk driving arrests and charges.

Winning "A Proactive Approach to Assault/Domestic Violence"

Judge's Take: The judges of Washtenaw County handle domestic violence and assault cases with great care, because there is an alleged victim on the other side of the case. Because of this, a judge is going to be very careful to protect the victim and monitor the person charged with these offenses.

One difference with an assault case vs another type of charge is a judge in Washtenaw County is likely to put a no contact order in place, which is a court order for the person charged to not contact the alleged victim either directly or by a third party. If this condition is violated, the offender will likely spend time in jail, or have a very high bond set to remain out of jail along with a tether on their ankle.

A judge views a domestic violence case as if there are three sides versus two, like most other cases. It's common for the alleged victim to appear in court with the judge interacting with the victim and the Defendant together.

It's common in a domestic violence case for either the Defendant or both the Defendant and the alleged victim to both want the no-contact order lifted, because the Defendant wants to return to the home. When it comes to finances and kids, it is difficult for one parent to be barred from the home, and even from having contact with the alleged victim.

In Washtenaw County, some judges will consider lifting this order more so than others, but if possible, I encourage my client that they are safer and in a better legal position to keep the no contact order in place. I am usually dealing with a client who has had his spouse, girlfriend, boyfriend, friend or family member call the police on them; a lot of times true or not, my client tells me they did nothing wrong, or this person lied about the incident.

My response is, if this is true, why would you want to put yourself back in that same position where not only will they call the police and have you arrested, but now you're also violating court orders, and likely putting yourself in a position to go to jail and have a criminal record.

When possible, I tell my clients to stay out of the house; sometimes this is unavoidable and we make a compelling request to the judge to lift the order. No matter our direction. my client is already being proactive from day one to impress upon the judge that they are already making changes in their life, and have the tools in place to avoid this incident.

Prosecutor's Take: The Washtenaw County Prosecutor's Office handles the majority of domestic violence cases in the County, and most of the assault cases. Of all the prosecutors I deal with in my practice, the Washtenaw County Prosecutor's Office is the toughest on domestic violence cases. It is a hot topic in Washtenaw County, and the policies set by the prosecutor are quite tough. They will also oppose all requests to have a non-contact order lifted.

The Prosecutor's Office regularly blocks dismissals from happening, which would be processed in other counties. If ANY prior threats or violence can be detected between the defendant and the victim, and this is anything but the first argument between these two people, the County will not agree to any possibility of a dismissal.

In order to soften that stance, my clients undergo a proactive plan from day one, which usually opens the door a bit more with the prosecutor.

The problem with working with a prosecutor on these cases is they always just assume the client is guilty. When I was a prosecutor in New York and Michigan, I would look at a domestic violence case, and just assume that the Defendant was guilty and the victim was truly an innocent victim. Even if the alleged victim tries to recant their story, I would blame this on the victim forgiving the Defendant, and needing them back in the life, and without a criminal record.

In Washtenaw County, the prosecutor will not dismiss the case because the victim no longer wants to prosecute. The prosecutor assumes the role as the protector of the victim, and is actually the one charging the

Defendant, not the victim; the victim is simply a witness, and not a party. Many times, my client and I are forced to set the case for trial, because that is the only way to get a case dismissed in Washtenaw County.

If the victim does not show up for trial, because the prosecutor could not issue a subpoena, or one was issued, but the victim ignored it, the prosecutor will ask for an adjournment. The judge may grant an adjournment, and if the victim again fails to show, the case will be dismissed. Some judges may dismiss the case the first time the victim does not show up in court for a trial.

<u>Being Proactive:</u> As stated above, it is difficult to get a domestic violence case dismissed in Washtenaw County. Assault cases without the domestic element while not as tough, are also very difficult to resolve. Because the climate is so tough, my clients undergo my intensive proactive program.

It's common for alcohol to be involved in domestic violence cases; this goes for both the Defendant and the victim. So from day one, my client is not going to drink alcohol during their case, and if we're asking for the client to return home, my client is already testing for alcohol, and we can argue from a strong position that the judge should not be concerned about alcohol consumption leading to more bad behavior.

Alcohol can sometimes actually help a domestic violence case, because we can stress that without the alcohol this doesn't happen, and if we take alcohol out of the equation then there should no longer be any issues. If drugs are involved, we address this head on with proactive drug testing.

Along with alcohol testing, I have my clients enroll in an intensive domestic violence program from day one; these programs can be 26 or 52 weeks and are viewed as quite challenging. If you're sentenced for domestic violence in Washtenaw County, you're likely to have to complete one of these programs instead of going to jail.

If the prosecutor is not willing to agree to a dismissal, having my client already working on the domestic violence program can change that stance in a hurry. There is no downside to enrolling in the program; it does not make you guilty or look guilty. It makes you look like that you understand domestic violence is serious, and you're not someone who engages in that type of violence. By taking the classes, you're giving yourself the education and tools to avoid future incidents.

A prosecutor is going to be very impressed with your proactive efforts, and if they are going to dismiss your case, it's not because they think you're innocent, it's because they believe you've learned your lesson, and will not engage in this type of behavior again. There is no better way to convince a prosecutor of that than by starting the race.

In simple terms, the prosecutor is not allowing you to sign up for the New York City Marathon, because they don't think you'll even show, and if you do, you still won't be able to handle the grueling race. Well what if you surprised the prosecutor by not only showing up, and starting the race, but you're already half-way done and making tremendous progress; wouldn't that help your argument? That's exactly what being proactive is all about in Washtenaw County.

Winning "A Proactive Approach to Youth Offenses"

Judge's Take: I define "youth offenses" as MIP's, Fake ID, Urinating in Public, Disorderly Conduct and Noise violations. I see most of these cases at the 15th District Court in Ann Arbor, and the cases are handled by Judge Valvo and Judge Hines.

These crimes usually involve alcohol consumption and fall under the umbrella of "youth offenses". The judges in Washtenaw County don't view you as a criminal because you peed in public or had a fake ID with you, but they need to act upon these crimes in a way, which a clear message is sent to the person charged. These are all misdemeanors, and if you plead guilty or are found guilty of these offenses, you will have a criminal record.

There is no better way to kill your career and goals in life than having an MIP on your record, even though it's no longer a criminal offense in 2018. A lot of people overlook how bad a Urinating in Public (UIP) and fake ID charge look on a record. Employers are going to assume the UIP is some sort of public indecency/sex offense. They will see the fake ID as possession of altered or fraudulent documents; there is no indication that you were really just trying to buy beer at a bar with this ID; instead the the perception is fraud and deception, and the future employer will think you stole the answer key for some exam, or something worse. These two offenses are probably worse than an MIP in a background check, because it is all about perception.

When a Washtenaw County judge handles one of these types of cases, it's not so much the actual offense they are concerned about; the concern comes from the pattern and predicting the future for the client. To judges, these are gateway offenses to worse offenses, and if the client is committing these offenses at such a young age, it could mean this person is out of control, and likely heading down the wrong path. Judges in Washtenaw County want to save young offenders, and may resort to jail, two years of probation, daily alcohol and drug testing, and putting a misdemeanor on your record as the ultimate wake-up call.

This is why all of my clients charged with these types of offenses go on my proactive plan from day one.

Prosecutor's Take: The majority of these types of cases are handled by the City of Ann Arbor, and not the Washtenaw County Prosecutor's office, and that is a good thing. The prosecutor, like the judges are not looking to ruin someone's life over an isolated incident, but it needs to be just that; an isolated incident, which needs to stop.

A young offender has a lot of potential to cause more trouble down the road; it's quite common that a prosecutor gets to know the names of certain young offenders who simply keep getting into trouble. How is a prosecutor able to determine the isolated incidents, and the offenses, which are the beginning of a pattern of bad behavior. A prosecutor may decide to take a tough stance on day one in order to send a message, and avoid further problems with this person; go light early, and the offender may keep trying to game the system.

Because the prosecutor doesn't know anything about the client other than the charge, my client and I get to work early on my proactive program. After reviewing my client's accomplishments and comparing them with other offenders, it becomes quite clear that my client is different, and is likely to be the offender who will not return to court with more trouble in the future. Prosecutors like a judge, are looking to make sure the right message is sent, and balance is found in the outcome. If my client can come to court already having completed a number of proactive measures, those actions speak louder than any possible words.

Being Proactive: When I work with a young person on their case, even a first offender lacks experience and a track record. It's like submitting a resume for a job; this person is not a known quantity, and it's too unpredictable to give them benefit of the doubt. If a 20-year-old has never been in trouble before, that means very little to a judge and prosecutor; they simply lacked the opportunity to get in trouble.

Compare this with a 45-year-old showing up in court with no criminal record; that's like having 25-years more work experience than the 20-year-old; the 45-year-old has earned the trust of the prosecutor and the court in a limited way, and is usually given the benefit of the doubt. It's a lot easier to say the 45-year-old's incident is isolated than the 20-year-old.

Because of this perception, my client and I need to fill in the blanks on the resume. We can't make the client older, but we can add multiple actions to show who the client is, and what they are likely to do in the future. Being proactive takes away some of that unpredictability; like my example of starting the marathon on your own if the organizers aren't sure you'll even show up; just start the race, and waive to them half-way through the race.

The most important thing to address in cases is alcohol use. Showing that the client understands that underage drinking is against the law, and although not the crime of the century, they understand that they found themselves in court, because of it. MIP cases are sometimes viewed as DUI cases that ended early; the underage client could have easily jumped in a car or ended up hurting themselves or someone else, because of the alcohol use. Even though no longer a criminal offense in Michigan, most people charged with this offense, will be applying for college, graduate school and jobs in other states, which still consider it a crime.

We address the elephant in the room and engage in alcohol education, along with an impact component of attending a few AA meetings. My clients also perform proactive community service to show that they are a positive influence in the community, and not someone who is going to be a negative influence going forward. It's all about actions, and showing how you have reacted since the offense occurred. If you sit back, and do nothing, what does the prosecutor and judge know about you other than the offense?

If you come to court showing you've attended alcohol classes, went to an AA meeting, and completed 20 hours of community service, doesn't it make sense that the judge and prosecutor will focus on those actions, and less on the criminal charge? Some clients are concerned that doing these things before going to court make them look guilty, well I have news for you, you are likely very guilty, and that's ok. Just because you broke the law, it doesn't mean you have to be punished for it like everyone else. You have the opportunity to be different, and if you're willing to voluntarily acknowledge your bad judgment, a judge and prosecutor are happy to put you in the "willing to learn from it, second chance" column rather than an adversarial punishment column.

If you've been charged with one of these offenses in Washtenaw County, and you're willing to be proactive from day one, there is a good chance that we can work with the judge and prosecutor on having your case resolved in a manner which does not leave you with a criminal record.

CHAPTER FIVE

COMMON MISDEMEANORS AND FELONIES

The Michigan Penal Code and Michigan Vehicle Code have thousands of offenses, which a person in Michigan can be charged, but we're only going to discuss the most common offenses. I'll go offense by offense, and discuss the different ways, which you can approach each offense, and some comments about how my proactive plan is quite effective for each offense. I will also make some comments about how each offense may be handled differently in some of the courts around Washtenaw County.

If the crime you or someone you care about is not listed in this chapter, it doesn't mean there isn't a comprehensive game plan to follow and succeed. It just means it's not one of the more common offense that I handle, but I would encourage you to reach out to me to hear my thoughts, and we can go from there.

If you're looking for my thoughts on drunk driving offenses, then I have dedicated an entire chapter to these offenses, which you can find later in this book. Additionally, I have also dedicated an entire chapter to what I call "tailgate offenses" such as Minor in Possession, Fake ID, Urinating in Public and other similar offenses, which you can also find later in this book.

Retail Fraud - First, Second & Third Degree

Michigan Retail Fraud requires the prosecution to prove beyond a reasonable doubt that my client did the following:

- the defendant took some property that the store offered for sale,
- the defendant moved the property (Any movement is enough. It does not matter whether the defendant actually got the property past the cashier or out of the store)
- the defendant intended to steal the property. Intended to steal means that the defendant intended to permanently take the property from the store without the store's consent.

- this happened either inside the store or in the immediate area around the store, while the store was open to the public.
- the value of the property

If the value of the property is below $200, it is Michigan Retail Fraud in Third Degree, which is a 93 day misdemeanor.

If the value of the property is between $200-$1,000, it is Michigan Retail Fraud in Second Degree, which is a one year misdemeanor.

If the value of the property is more than $1,000, it is Michigan Retail Fraud in the First Degree, which is a felony.

The most common retail fraud offenses in Washtenaw County are third and second degree, which are handled in the district courts. I see retail fraud cases mostly at the 14A-1 District Court with Judge Conlin and either the Washtenaw County Prosecutor's Office or the Pittsfield Township as the prosecutor, and at the 15th District Court in downtown Ann Arbor with the County or the City of Ann Arbor.

Retail fraud in Washtenaw County is a crime of theft, fraud and dishonesty, and having it on your record will likely cost you a current job and future job opportunities. My proactive program puts my clients in a position to show that this was an isolated moment in time. Between educational classes, support groups and community service work, my client is able to change the story of their case and usually able to convince the prosecutor and judge to consider dismissing their charges. This is an extraordinary result, which must be earned while following a comprehensive plan.

Another route to take is simply to go to trial and challenge the evidence. Your defense typically comes down to the lack of intent to steal the items in question. Maybe you forgot something was in your cart, or maybe you had to run outside because you forgot something in the car, or your child needed to leave the store for an emergency. If you have items with you, and you don't pay under these circumstances, and other similar facts, you may not be guilty. It will come down to your word vs the word of the store employees. Unfortunately if you're found guilty at trial, you will likely not be able to receive any sort of dismissal consideration as that opportunity has passed. Retail fraud cases are a balancing act between the pros and cons of various options, but ultimately my goal for any client is to avoid a conviction and jail.

Domestic Violence & Aggravated Domestic Violence

Michigan domestic violence is a reality, and it touches every age, gender and socioeconomic group. If you've been charged with domestic violence in Michigan, it's important that you have an advocate in your corner from the very beginning. Michigan domestic violence affects every aspect of your life, and it can carry life altering consequences.

Your attorney will gather all of the evidence in your case, and get a private investigator involved if necessary. Based on this investigation, you and your attorney will build your defense, and our first goal will be an outright dismissal or a not guilty verdict at trial. While building up your defense, your attorney will engage in negotiations with the prosecuting attorney, to develop various backup plans. It may also be possible to have a conversation with the judge in your case, and get an indication of what your possible sentence might be. All of this will be very important in deciding the path of your case.

To be found guilty of domestic violence in Michigan, it must be proven beyond a reasonable doubt that you assaulted or battered one of the following:

#1 - A spouse, a former spouse, a person which you share a child in common, a resident or former resident of your household or a person which you have or had a dating relationship.

#2- A battery is a forceful, violent, or offensive touching of a person or something closely connected with him or her. The touching must have been intended by the defendant, that is, not accidental, and it must have been against the victim's will.

An assault is an attempt to commit a battery or an act that would cause a reasonable person to fear or apprehend an immediate battery. The defendant must have intended either to commit a battery or to make the victim reasonably fear an immediate battery. An assault cannot happen by accident. At the time of an assault, the defendant must have had the ability to commit a battery, or must have appeared to have the ability, or must have thought he/she had the ability.

A domestic violence charge becomes "aggravated" and goes from a 93 day misdemeanor to a one year misdemeanor if the victim required medical attention at the time or immediately after the incident. If you have prior domestic violence convictions, you can be charged as a second offender (one year misdemeanor), and a third offender (felony).

As a domestic violence first offender, you may also be eligible to a plea guilty as a first offender, but have the case dismissed after a period of time. This plea bargain falls under MCL 769.4A, and is only available to Michigan domestic violence first time offenders.

Unfortunately this first offender outcome is not offered in Washtenaw County very often, because this type of plea bargain requires consent by the prosecutor and the victim, and will require an admission of guilt or a plea of no-contest. In Washtenaw County, the prosecutor doesn't agree to this outcome, except in some rare cases.

The other option for a domestic violence case in Washtenaw County is setting your case for trial. If the victim does not appear for court, the prosecutor may need to dismiss the case, but the Washtenaw County Prosecutor's Office is very good at getting the victim to court under court order of a subpoena or a material witness warrant, which essentially means arresting the witness so they have to appear in court.

In Michigan domestic violence cases, the prosecution can also bring in statements of the victim made to the police about your case; this is unique to domestic violence cases. This exception for domestic violence is important to the prosecution, because the victim for a number of reasons may or may not testify to the complete story or even recant, but this exception allows the police to testify as to what the victim stated at an earlier date. This essentially allows the prosecution to have a backup plan in case the victim cannot provide the testimony needed for a conviction. This special rule for domestic violence cases makes a trial more challenging that most other offenses.

Another thing that makes a domestic violence trial unique is that the prosecution is entitled to introduce additional evidence that you as the charged party have committed domestic violence in the past. This could stem from another case, an arrest or even events that were never reported to the police. The prosecution can have the victim in the present case testify to past events and/or victims from your past. With Michigan domestic violence comes the possibility of manipulation and ulterior motives.

Washtenaw County is the worst county in the area to be charged with domestic violence. It will require a deep dedication to a proactive plan, because you are not granted any benefit of the doubt in, it is something you need to earn through action over time. You need to demonstrate that you're not using alcohol or drugs, that you're educating yourself on avoiding future incidents, and you're being a productive and safe member of society; someone who deserves to go forward without a violent criminal record.

I see most domestic violence cases in Washtenaw County at the 15th District Court, which are all handled by Judge Hines, and at the 14A-3 court in Chelsea, which are handled by Judge Conlin. Both of these courts will have the Washtenaw County Prosecutor's Office as the prosecutor, which makes things quite challenging. Fortunately for my clients, both Judge Hines and Conlin are open to clients receiving education and treatment instead of jail if they demonstrate a proactive step in the right direction from day one. My proactive plan is geared toward anticipating what each judge is looking for, and we aim to satisfy these expectations before even going to court for the first time.

Drug Offenses - Misdemeanor & Felony Possession

When someone contacts me for a drug offense in Washtenaw County, it's important for me to learn a lot more about their background. I have clients who have never been in trouble with the law before, and have some marijuana in their dorm room on campus, then I have clients who are driving around with a long criminal history of drug use, and they are found with large quantities of prescription drugs.

There are a number of Michigan controlled substance crimes. There are levels of controlled substances: Schedule 1 through Schedule 5. Here is a breakdown of the different offenses, and what the prosecution must prove beyond a reasonable doubt.

If you do not have a previous drug conviction, you may be eligible for 7411 under the Michigan Public Health Code, which allows for a deferral (keep conviction off record) for first time drug offenders, but this is something you must earn from the prosecutor and the judge. Here are the most common drug offenses for first offenders:

Unlawful Possession of a Controlled Substance with Intent to Deliver

- First, that the defendant knowingly possessed a controlled substance.
- Second, that the defendant intended to deliver this substance to someone else.
- Third, that the substance possessed was ___________ and the defendant knew it was.
- Fourth, that the substance was in a mixture that weighed (state weight).
- Fifth, that the defendant was not legally authorized to possess this substance.

Unlawful Possession of a Controlled Substance

- First, that the defendant possessed a controlled substance.
- Second, that the substance possessed was ___________.
- Third, that the defendant knew that [he/she] was possessing [list substance].

- Fourth, that the substance was in a mixture that weighed (state weight).
- Fifth, that the substance was not obtained by a valid prescription given to the defendant.
- Sixth, that the defendant was not otherwise authorized to possess this substance.

Unlawful Use of a Controlled Substance
- Prosecution must prove:
- First, that the defendant used a controlled substance.
- Second, that the substance used was __________.
- Third, that at the time [he / she] used it, the defendant knew the substance was __________.
- Fourth, that the substance was not obtained by a valid prescription given to the defendant.
- Fifth, that the defendant was not otherwise authorized by law to use this substance.

As noted above, if you're a first offender for some drug offense, you may be eligible for a first offender program, but this still means likely one year of probation, daily drug and alcohol testing, treatment and education, and other sanctions, which any violation will leave you with a criminal record, and jail time. My clients always consider this option if they are eligible, but we also explore other options, which may allow us to avoid a conviction in a different manner.

Even if you earn this exceptional result, you still need to avoid trouble for a year, pass all drug tests, attend any counseling and/or treatment, and if you have any slipups, the conviction goes on your record, and you're likely to go to jail. The goal is to minimize the requirements and length of time to complete this process. It's the difference between needing to get all A's at Harvard over four years with getting a set of B's at community service for a semester. Probation does not need to be difficult or time consuming if you're proactive from day one.

My clients are proactive from day one, which means proactive drug and alcohol testing, a substance abuse screening and assessment, and follow the recommendation, along with proactive community service. If my clients follow my lead, we may be able to get a first offender program, but only three months probation vs twelve months, with no requirements to fulfill, because everything has been done already. The requirements were done ahead of time without the penalty of going to jail and having a criminal record over their head.

I see misdemeanor drug cases most commonly at the 15th District Court, which are handled by Judge Valvo and Hines, and at the 14A-4 District Court in Saline, which is handled by Judge Simpson.

As for common felony drug offenses, the most common is felony possession of an analogue, which is essentially a prescription drug, which you don't have a prescription for, which is actually a felony in Michigan. I have clients driving and walking around with prescription pills, which they don't have a valid prescription for, and they end up with felony charges.

If you're charged with felony possession in Washtenaw County, your case will be set for a Preliminary Examination Conference, followed by a Preliminary Examination. Your case can be resolved at this stage, which takes place at the 14A-1 District Court, or the case may proceed to the Washtenaw County Circuit Court for further proceedings and trial.

A client charged with felony possession undergoes a similar proactive plan as a client charged with a misdemeanor, with one major exception. I typically encourage my client charged with a felony to enroll and complete and intensive outpatient treatment program. It may seem over the top, but if a judge and prosecutor are worried about my client having a major drug issues, we might as well take the air out of the 800 pound elephant in the room, and just complete the treatment. From there, major drug issue or not, we've at least educated ourselves, and were treated in the eyes of the prosecutor and judge.

Following this path typically leads to a dismissal, and no jail or prison, because my client took the path of learning from their case, rather than needing to be punished into learning from it. It's important to take a felony possession case out of the punishment column, because prison time is possible, and enter the column of treatment and education.

Assaultive Crimes in Washtenaw County

Assaultive crimes in Washtenaw County are assault crimes that are not considered domestic violence. Assault crimes can be between friends, co-workers, strangers etc; anyone who does not have a romantic or domestic (living together) element attached to it.

Assault crimes in Washtenaw County are handled very carefully, and are generally handled by the Washtenaw County Prosecutor's Office, which really works with their victims on determining any plea deals. If the victim is willing to reduce charges then it generally happens; if the victim is not willing to reduce, then it doesn't happen.

If any injuries were caused, which resulted in medical bills, the prosecutor will typically seek financial restitution from my client. If the amount is something we disagree with, the client is entitled to a restitution hearing.

Depending upon the facts of the case, the Washtenaw County Prosecutor's Office may be willing to offer a special program, which could result in your charges being dismissed upon successful completion of probation, but this is a rare outcome, which must be earned by my client.

The majority of the assault cases that I see come from the 15th District Court in Ann Arbor and the 14A-1 District Court in Pittsfield Township. Judge Hines handles all the assault cases in Ann Arbor, and Judge Conlin would handle the case in Pittsfield Township.

Here are the four most common crimes for first offenders:

(1) **Michigan Simple Assault & Battery,** which is defined under MCL 750.81

A person who assaults or assaults and batters an individual, if no other punishment is prescribed by law, is guilty of a misdemeanor punishable by imprisonment for not more than 93 days or a fine of not more than $500.00, or both."

In Michigan, a battery is defined as a forceful, violent, or offensive touching of the person or something closely connected with the person of another. The touching must have been intended by the defendant, that is, not accidental, and it must have been against that person's will. It does not matter whether the touching caused an injury. If a battery does not occur, it's still possible to have committed an assault, which is an act that would cause a reasonable person to fear or apprehend an immediate battery.

A few important questions that my clients explore:
- Was the touching an accident?
- Was the touching done with consent of the other party or was there an implied consent?
- Was the touching mutual?

(2) **Michigan Aggravated Assault**, which is defined under MCL 750.81a(1)

A Michigan Simple Assault becomes an Aggravated Assault when the victim suffers an injury. The Prosecution will usually have to prove this injury with medical records or proof of medical treatment. A person who assaults an individual without a weapon and inflicts serious or aggravated injury upon that individual without intending to commit murder or to inflict great bodily harm less than murder is guilty of a misdemeanor punishable by imprisonment for not more than 1 year or a fine of not more than $1,000.00, or both."

Serious injury for purposes of the aggravated assault statute has been defined as a physical injury that requires immediate medical treatment or that causes disfigurement, impairment of health, or impairment of a part of the body. It's important that your attorney has the opportunity to evaluate the extent of the alleged injury. It's possible that an Michigan Aggravated Assault could be reduced to a Simple Assault depending upon the facts of your case.

(3) **Michigan Felonious Assault (Assault with a Dangerous Weapon),** defined under MCL 750.82(1)

A Felonious Assault is a Simple Assault, but the assault was committed with a dangerous weapon. A person who assaults another person with a dangerous weapon without intending to commit murder or to inflict great bodily harm less than murder is guilty of a felony punishable by imprisonment for not more than 4 years or a fine of not more than $2,000.00, or both.

The elements of felonious assault are (1) an assault, (2) with a dangerous weapon, and (3) with the intent to injure or place the victim in reasonable apprehension of an immediate battery. Because felonious assault includes an "assault" as an element, there must be a present ability or apparent present ability to commit a battery in order to be convicted of felonious assault.

The most frequently asked question:
What exactly constitutes a dangerous weapon?

Past court cases have made the following, but not limited to distinctions:

Dangerous weapon: Automobile, beer bottle, shoe, unloaded gun, tear gas spray, shoe, high heel, lighter fluid, flashlight, dog, broomstick, booted foot, aerosol spray can, frying pan

Non-dangerous weapon: human teeth, bare hands

It's important that you speak to your attorney about the circumstances of your case, and to closely examine the alleged dangerous weapon. If the alleged weapon is something of value or sentimental meaning (family knife or antique firearm), it's likely that the weapon used in this offense may or may not be returned upon the completion of your case; your attorney can work with the judge in coming to this decision.

(4) **Michigan Assault with Intent to do Great Bodily Harm**, which is defined under MCL 750.84

"Any person who shall assault another with intent to do great bodily harm, less than the crime of murder, shall be guilty of a felony punishable by imprisonment in the state prison not more than 10 years, or by a fine of not more than 5,000 dollars."

Assault with intent to commit great bodily harm less than murder requires proof of (1) an attempt or threat with force or violence to do corporal harm to another (an assault), and (2) an intent to do great bodily harm less than murder.

The term "intent to do great bodily harm less than the crime of murder" is an intent to do serious injury of an aggravated nature. No physical injury is required for the elements of the crime to be established. It's important to understand that the resulting injury from this offense is less important than the "potential injury".

If you're charged to have kicked, punched and beaten someone repeatedly upon their face and body, but the end result was a minor injury, the "potential injury" allows you to be charged with this serious offense. The "what if" is defined as a physical injury that could seriously harm the health or function of the body. The Prosecution will generally have to elicit testimony during trial to establish the "potential injury".

The first two crimes I listed are misdemeanors, which are handled in the district courts, and the last two are felonies handled first at the 14A-1 Court in Pittsfield Township for Preliminary Examination Conference and Preliminary Examination. The misdemeanor offenses typically result in probation, but some people do go to jail for misdemeanor assault cases in Washtenaw County. The felony charges typically result in jail or prison, and the prosecutor is less likely to consider any dismissal program.

Having an assault crime on your record, either a misdemeanor or a felony can ruin your career, and your life. It's important from day one to make the decision to change the perception of your case. The prosecutor, judge, the police department and your community view you as a dangerous person who hurts people, even to the level of seriously injuring or killing them.

It may have been self defense, a misunderstanding, or you simply had the worst day of your life. No matter why this happened, you can't allow others to control your case, and the outcome of the case. You have the opportunity to be proactive, and create the outcome you deserve; your goals may be avoiding jail and/or a criminal conviction. Both of these are possible if you're willing to follow a comprehensive program and earn these results.

Resisting Arrest in Washtenaw County

If you've been charged with Resisting Arrest in Washtenaw County, this doesn't make you a criminal or a bad person. I see clients on a daily basis who have have never been involved with the police and have never hurt a person in their life. It's quite common that a good person will get themselves in a bad situation, which results in being charged with Resisting Arrest.

Resisting Arrest is defined as "an individual who assaults, batters, wounds, resists, obstructs, opposes or endangers a person who the individual knows or has reason to know is performing his or her duties". Resisting arrest in Michigan is a felony that carries a penalty of two years in person. I also have clients who are charged with similar sounding offenses at the 15th District Court under a City of Ann Arbor local ordinance, and not state law, which is a misdemeanor.

General rule of thumb for Resisting Arrest is if you're charged by the City of Ann Arbor it is always a misdemeanor, but if charged by Washtenaw County Prosecutor's Office, it's a felony.

If you're charged by the City of Ann Arbor, and during the incident the police officer is injured and requires immediate medical attention, the offense is a four year felony. If the police officer suffers a serious impairment of a body function, the offense is now a 15 year felony, and if the incident causes death to a police officer, it is now a 20 year felony.

It is becoming more common for prosecutors in Michigan to charge resisting arrest in cases where the charge may not have been issued in the past. One could argue that most arrests in Michigan have some aspect of either resisting, obstructing or opposing, but the crime is not always charged. Some prosecutors will cut the defendant a break, and only charge attempted resisting arrest, which makes the crime a misdemeanor rather than a felony.

Another common charging strategy is to charge a bunch of misdemeanors along with felony resisting arrest, with the idea that dismissing the felony will be a bargaining chip to get the client to plead guilty to the other misdemeanors. While a dismissal of the felony is a great result, having a series of misdemeanors on your record may not allow you to expunge your record at a later date, and leave you with a permanent criminal record.

When I work with a client who is charged with Resisting Arrest, the first thing we need to overcome is the perception that my client does not respect law enforcement, which is likely not true. In Washtenaw County, the police and prosecutor doesn't typically jam up clients with a felony like Resisting Arrest unless the client really gives the police a problem. The client is typically intoxicated, or very upset about something unrelated to the police. Basically, but for the alcohol or the situation, my client would not have acted in this manner toward the police. It's easy to say that, but how does the prosecutor, police and judge know that? It's our job to be proactive and show all parties who my client really is; and this has to happen on day one.

I will have clients address alcohol concerns with attendance at AA, alcohol education and/or treatment, alcohol and drug testing, and possibly anger management classes. This may seem like a lot to some potential clients, but if you want to give yourself every opportunity to avoid a felony, you will agree to this all-out sprint in order to avoid the marathon of going through life with a felony criminal record. One month of being proactive and bettering yourself is worth it.

Careless/Reckless Driving in Washtenaw County

If you have been charged with either Reckless or Careless Driving in Washtenaw County, it's important to know what the prosecution must prove. If charged with either offense, most jurisdictions will offer a plea to a lesser charge, but if the prosecution cannot prove the charge, why should you plea? You should not plea to either offense if facing a weak case, because both crimes carry substantial driving sanctions for your Michigan driver's license license.

If you're charged with reckless or careless driving, and you are not offered a plea then you should most certainly challenge the charge. These two offenses can have a major impact on your driver's license, and could sink you financially.

Like any other offense in Washtenaw County, a client charged with either offense should be proactive from day one. It's important to explore what caused these alleged offenses to occur, and to address any concerns. I've worked with clients who have fallen asleep at the wheel or had a medical emergency, but were still charged with these offenses. Beyond showing the prosecutor and judge what happened, it's also about addressing the question: will it happen again?

Along with addressing underlying issues, there's also an opportunity to show a prosecutor and judge that the client has learned from the incident, and moving forward will be a better and safer driver. This usually means exploring driver improvement/safe-driving courses, which can not only make you a better driver, but shows the prosecutor and judge that you proactively sought this out, and you're generally as concerned as they are about the alleged bad driving.

With all "erratic" driving offenses in Michigan, you need to overcome the "asshole factor". As a former prosecutor, anytime I handled a case of someone charged with driving "erratically" on the highway, I reflected on my own experience of being annoyed by a driver, who I thought was driving like an asshole. I was not exactly willing to cut this person a break, because I made a general assumption about their case.

From being in the position of once stereotyping these drivers, I created a proactive plan for my clients to overcome that assumption. If back in my day as a prosecutor, an attorney came to me and showed the client had no prior driving offenses, this was an isolated incident, and the client has already addressed any concerns about poor driving by proactively completing a driver improvement class, I would be willing to dismiss and/or reduce charges.

Nobody ever did that, so I do it now, and it works. Here are more specific breakdowns of the two offenses, and what a prosecutor must prove in court:

Reckless Driving

To found guilty of this offense, the prosecution must show that you were driving a car on a road open to the public or generally accessible to cars, including a parking lot, and you drove the car in a willful or wanton disregard for the safety of persons or property. "Willful or wanton disregard" means more than simple carelessness but does not require proof of an intent to cause harm. It means knowingly disregarding the possible risks to the safety of people or property.

This offense is a 90-day misdemeanor and carries many of the same license implications, fines and costs of a drunk driving offense. If convicted of this offense, six points would be added to your license.
The prosecution will attempt to prove this charge with testimony of your driving, including speed, along with the the road conditions. If

there is evidence of intoxication, the prosecution will be allowed to introduce this evidence; the jury may factor this into the decision whether there was a "willful or wanton disregard" for the safety or persons or property, but this alone is not enough for a conviction.

One way to defeat a reckless driving charge is to show an error in judgment on the part of the charged driver to explain the erratic driving, which creates reasonable doubt as "willful or wanton disregard". Let's say you're observed switching lanes, which causes an accident, and you're charged with reckless driving - well if the other car was in your blind spot, then this may be merely negligence on your part, not willful disregard.

Careless Driving

Careless Driving requires the prosecution to prove you drove in a careless, imprudent or negligent manner. Reckless requires you intentionally drove in a certain manner, whereas Careless doesn't look to your willful disregard but rather the results of your driving.

Careless driving carries the possibility of three points on your license, but it is not a misdemeanor, and carries no possible jail time. The fines, costs and license implications are less severe than Reckless Driving.

A careless driving case has a lower burden for the prosecution. Depending on the facts in your case, it's possible that the other driver was at fault, or your driving decision was out of necessity such as to avoid another car, a pot hole or any other reasonable explanation.

Larceny Charges in Washtenaw County

A lot of clients and attorneys don't quite understand the difference between Larceny and Retail Fraud, because many courts and prosecutors use both terms for the same types of offenses. The general rule is stealing from a retail store is Retail Fraud/Shoplifting, while stealing something that is not for sale is a form of larceny.

If the Washtenaw County Prosecutor's Office charges you with larceny, it is not the same as Retail Fraud. If one of the local city or township prosecutors, charges you with larceny, it could be a "Retail Fraud" dressed up with a different name. You know the facts of your case, if they are saying you stole an item that was for sale it means one thing, if you took something from somewhere or someone that wasn't for sale it means another. We will be able to easily determine the nature of charges once we go over the facts of your case.

We've already addressed Retail Fraud offenses, so let's discuss other theft crimes. I put a similar proactive plan into place that I do for Retail Fraud cases, but with a tweak on the educational class, which is geared less toward a possible shoplifting addiction, and more toward positive life adjustment.

The first theft crime is **Michigan Larceny by Conversion**, which the prosecution must prove beyond a reasonable doubt that:

- the property of another was delivered to the defendant
- the defendant converted the property to his own use
- at the time of conversion, the defendant intended to defraud or cheat the owner permanently
- the conversion was without owner's consent

The second theft crime is **Michigan Larceny from an Automobile**, which the prosecution must prove beyond a reasonable doubt that

- the defendant took something from the car
- the property was taken without consent
- the property was in or on the car
- there was some movement of the property (doesn't matter if defendant kept property)
- at the time of property taken, defendant intended to permanently deprive owner.

The third theft crime is **Michigan Larceny from a Person**, which the prosecution must prove beyond a reasonable doubt that

- the defendant took the property of another
- the property was taken without consent
- there was movement of the property
- at the time of taking, it was taken from person's immediate control or presence
- intention was to permanently deprive owner of property

The fourth theft crime is **Michigan Larceny from a Building**, which the prosecution must prove beyond a reasonable doubt that

- the defendant took someone else's property
- the property was taken without consent
- the property was taken from a building

- there was some movement of the property (doesn't matter if defendant kept or left with it)
- the property was worth something at the time it was taken
- the defendant intended to permanently deprive owner of the property

Some other theft offenses include:

Michigan Larceny by Trick, which involves the defendant having some limited, special or temporary purpose for possession property, but owner never intended in handing over full-time ownership. During temporary ownership, the defendant does something that defendant knew was not party of agreement and takes property without consent.

Receiving and Concealing Stolen Property, which states a person shall not buy, receive, possess, conceal, or aid in the concealment of stolen, embezzled, or converted money, goods, or property knowing, or having reason to know or reason to believe, that the money, goods, or property is stolen, embezzled, or converted. Depending upon the value of the goods, the crime could be a misdemeanor of a felony.

Malicious Destruction of Property in Washtenaw County

If you've been charged with Malicious Destruction of Property (MDOP) in Washtenaw, it's important to discuss what was damaged, whom the property belongs to, and why did this happen. I'd say 99.9 percent of the time, either alcohol or a feeling of anger or revenge were involved. It's quite rare that someone destroys the property of another for fun when they are sober.

Once we can address why this happened, the client is in a better position to show that incident was an isolated moment in time, and provide the reason it happened. It's not an excuse or a defense to the crime that you were highly intoxicated and angry at a boyfriend or girlfriend and smashed their car window, but it provides the reason. It shows you're not a terrible person who does this for fun or when you're sober. It shows you can control yourself going forward if you remove the alcohol, and get help with your anger issues.

Maybe you shouldn't drink alcohol for awhile, or attend AA, counseling and treatment for alcohol use, and anger management. Most clients agree that the alcohol was the reason, so we need to show an effort to take that element out of the mix, and also address anger in a different way than destroying property. If a client is willing to follow my lead, it is likely the client can pay for the damages, and have their case reduced or dismissed.

To go to jail and have a criminal record for one drunk moment in time, is not the equitable outcome, but you do not get the benefit of the doubt by simply ignoring the underlying issues.

In order to be found guilty of this offense, the prosecution must prove the following elements:

1- The property belonged to someone other than the defendant
2- The defendant destroyed or damaged the property
3- The defendant did so knowing it was wrong without just cause or excuse, and with intent to damage the property

4- Proving the amount of damage, which will determine what level offense you're charged with

- If the damage is under $200 dollars, you will be charged with a 93 day misdemeanor.
- If the damage is between $200-$1,000 dollars you will be charged with a one year misdemeanor
- If the damage exceeds $1,000, but below $20,000, you will be charged with a felony
- If the damage exceeds $20,000 you will be charged with a more serious felony that carries more jail time

The prosecution will be able to add together numerous incidents if the crime involved the same parties within 12 months. The test for value is "fair market value". This is what is called a specific intent crime, which means if the defendant did not purposely destroy the property, but rather did it by mistake or without intent, the prosecution cannot prove the case beyond a reasonable doubt, and the defendant is entitled to a not-guilty verdict.

CHAPTER SIX

TAILGATE OFFENSES IN WASHTENAW COUNTY

This chapter is specifically geared toward what I call "tailgate offenses" which typically happen most commonly on football weekends in Ann Arbor, but I handle these types of cases all over the County, and during different times of the year.

In Washtenaw County, and specifically Ann Arbor, the local police departments are mandated by their budget needs to issue hundreds and hundreds of tickets to students, residents and visitors of Ann Arbor. The tickets aren't issued because you're a bad person or even viewed as a criminal, but these offenses are all crimes, and will leave you with a criminal record. Too many people decide that they would prefer to take the shortcut and get the case over as soon as possible. They think that this is a minor offense, and if they plead guilty, they can move on with life. That mindset is extremely lazy and shortsighted, because a crime is a crime, and a misdemeanor is a misdemeanor.

When you're filling out an application, and it asks if you've been convicted of a crime, have a criminal record, or every been convicted of a crime, the answer to all of these popular questions is YES. You will not be admitted into schools, get a job, get loans or be allowed to chaperone your kid's field trip, because you have a criminal record.

The way I approach these common offenses is two-fold. The first thing we do is learn everything we can about the case, and what sort of evidence the prosecutor has to prosecute you. The second thing is for me to learn everything about you; your past, present and future goals. Although most people view these offenses as minor in nature, we still need to tackle the "trouble maker" syndrome. If you're charged with a "tailgate offense", it's likely you've committed this crime multiple times, and there is no reason for you to stop anytime soon.

If we can show the prosecutor and the judge, that you completely understand the consequences of the charges, and you've reacted by doing positive things in your life, and for the community, it's possible that a prosecutor will agree to reduce or dismiss the charges, and the judge will accept your proactive "punishment", and impose no further sanctions. In my experience, every one of these "tailgate offenses" can be resolved without any criminal record, but it takes time and effort. Most importantly, it requires calling a timeout, taking a step back, and fighting the temptation to plead guilty, or just do what everyone else is doing. The others know even less than you do, when they are making this rash decision to simply get the case over with; why follow them?

If you're the type of person that wants to have a comprehensive plan, set goals, and achieve those goals, I can help you avoid a criminal record.

I am going to cover five distinct offenses, which I call "tailgate offenses". There are others, but these five are the most common. I am also going to discuss them in context of the 15th District Court in Ann Arbor, as around 95 percent of these offenses occur in that area. Many of the concepts I discuss can be applied to any other court in Washtenaw County.

<u>Minor in Possession</u>

The year 2018 brings a change to the Minor in Possession law in Michigan.

Pre 2018, an MIP was a criminal misdemeanor, now a first offense is a civil infraction. This is under State of Michigan law, but most local cities, townships, villages and municipalities are sure to follow this change in the law.

When I speak to other defense lawyers, judges, prosecutors etc, all of them view this as a problem solving resolution, which is fair and equitable and everyone wins. While I agree decriminalizing Minor in Possession this is a good thing, there are far reaching unrecognized consequences to this change of the law. Handling this new civil infraction in a reckless manner will end up worse in the end than how it was treated under the old law.

Under the pre-2018 law, someone charged with minor in possession would usually go under a non-public deferment program, where the guilty plea would be withheld and never entered against the person. The case itself would not be public. Yes that person would be on probation and be subject to things like counseling, community service, alcohol testing etc, but in the end, nobody ever needs to know about it.

Under the new law, a judge can still order the defendant to participate in community service, alcohol testing and substance abuse treatment. Failure to comply will turn the case into a misdemeanor with little opportunity to avoid a criminal conviction.

Under the new law, young adults under 21 are going to view this as a get out of jail free card, and everyone gets to be caught once - no big deal?. This is going to lead to more irresponsible drinking, including binge drinking and more risk taking, including drunk driving, because the shortsighted end result in the mind of the young adult will be essentially a speeding ticket. They are both civil infractions yes, but let's think a bit outside the box.

Here's the problem, you don't want to walk into the courthouse and plead responsible to a Minor in Possession. Why? Because most states still consider it a criminal misdemeanor and it's a 100 percent public record for employers, graduate schools and the public to view.

You may think well it's not a crime anymore, so no big deal, well Fortune 500 companies and a law, business, nursing, medical or other graduate programs are going to run your public court record and see this offense, and will judge you based upon the result. Will it matter? Maybe; why take that chance?

Are they going to say applicant #1 has an MIP in Michigan, but applicant #2 has no record, but after researching it, it's a civil infraction, so it's ok, lets go with the first applicant? No, they are going to assume its a criminal offense, or still perceive it to be the same; in the end, they don't care how Michigan views the law.

The person viewing the offense may or may not know about how Michigan views it, and if they do, may not care.

When I was a prosecutor in NYC, we had a lower drunk driving offense that was not a criminal misdemeanor, but in the end, it's still drunk driving, and on a public record, the reader of the record is unlikely to make the distinction or care to make it, because it's the same set of circumstances - broadly drunk driving or in this case, possession of alcohol under the age of 21.

I am of the mindset that possession of alcohol for a minor is not the end of the world, and not "serious" in light of other offenses, but it's still a sign of poor decision making, not appreciating risk or contemplating the consequences of one's actions; that doesn't change because the legislature now calls it a civil infraction versus a misdemeanor. If I saw a driving record with 10 speeding tickets, all civil infractions, I would question that person's judgment on the road, despite it not being a criminal offense.

So here's what I'm doing with all of my clients who are charged with minor in possession in 2018 and beyond.

We're going to treat it like a criminal case in terms of obtaining all discovery, evidence and statements; just because it's no longer a crime, doesn't mean we're not going to pursue defenses and create leverage. We're going to be extremely proactive to address the poor decision that lead to this case, and educate and learn from it. If we take care of it upfront, easier to have the prosecutor and judge agree with our plan versus being told what the options are for the case.

We're going to set it for a formal hearing and not go plead guilty. Why just go plead guilty, what's the benefit?

Might as well set it for a hearing, make the officer show up and testify. In the end, if the prosecutor and police officer do 100 percent their job, you have the same result in the end. It's more likely the officer doesn't show, the prosecutor doesn't want to waste time on the hearing, or the officer doesn't remember such a "small incident" and can't provide the necessary proof to the court.

For most college town MIP cases, the officer is handing out 100's of tickets a day, do you really remember my clients case? Probably not.

What's going to end up happening is the prosecutor is going to be leveraged into offering something other than a minor in possession civil charge, which is what we want. So here are your options if charged with a first MIP in Michigan from 2018 and beyond.

1. Go plead responsible and put an MIP on your public record and do community service, counseling etc

or

2. Be proactive from day one, explore defenses, create leverage by having the opportunity to set a hearing, work toward a different resolution or hold the hearing and win; worse case, you end up with #1, and have a better chance of avoiding having to do the community service and counseling as part of a probation term.

Here's how things might play out with the prosecutor under the new law with this approach.

Me: So it's just a civil infraction now?

Me: Great, let's hold the formal hearing!!

Prosecutor: Whatttta mean?

Me: Let's hold it - your cop has no idea who jimmy, john or paul are, and can't remember each ticket

Prosecutor: Ughhhh, keep your voice down, don't want the other lawyers hearing this

Me: Let's really see if my client said X, Y or Z or if they really had alcohol in that cup, might as well, worst case, my client takes the civil infraction right?

Prosecutor: Crap, you didn't want to hold these when it was a misdemeanor, because losing meant a criminal record

Me: Right. Do you want to offer me something to avoid this hearing? Impeding? Littering?

Prosecutor: Ughhh, yeah I guess

For MIP cases in Ann Arbor, the judge will either be Judge Valvo or Hines, but it may be assigned to the magistrate to begin with for an arraignment. When I work with a client, we waive the arraignment, and ask for a court date with one of the judges. The prosecutor is usually the City of Ann Arbor as the Ann Arbor Police Department make most of the MIP arrests in Ann Arbor, but if the University of Michigan Police Department or the Sheriff's Office makes the arrest, the prosecutor will be the Washtenaw County Prosecutor's Office.

If my client has followed my lead with my proactive program, it's quite possible to get the judge and the prosecutor to join us in entering the educational/lesson learned column, and avoid the punishment column, while supporting our goal of not having a criminal record from this incident.

My clients create the outcome they want, and get the judge and the prosecutor to agree. We take control of the case, because by being proactive, you're showing that the case had the right impact on your life, and you earned the right to have your case dismissed. It's rare to control the outcome of your case when it comes to criminal law, but a proactive approach gives the client that unique power.

Fraudulent or Fake ID

Fake ID charges are usually associated with other charges such as an MIP, but this offense is a misdemeanor. The additional problem a client runs into with a Fake ID charge is the definition, which classifies it as a crime of dishonesty and fraud. The charge reads as if you possessed fraudulent documents, and you were looking to falsify and defraud someone; it's not clear that you had a friend's ID in your wallet, and you were going to a bar in Ann Arbor. Do you want a prospective employer or grad school to see that charge on your record?

Many clients who contact me about MIP charge, also tell me that the police found a fake ID during the arrest/ticketing process, and they now have multiple charges. This is quite common, as many people use Fake ID's to enter bars or purchase alcohol, and the crimes go hand-in-hand. This offense is a separate misdemeanor, which carries jail time, fines, costs and would leave you with a criminal record if convicted.

The main difference between an MIP charge, and a Fake ID charge comes down to the ability to keep it off of your record. In Michigan, there are built in ways to have an MIP off your record or dismissed at a later date, even a second one but this does NOT exist for the Fake ID charge. This is also a crime that is very easy to prove by the prosecutor, as it is in your wallet or you offer it to a bouncer or police officer as your identification. There is not much of a defense to it being in your wallet, or you handing it over.

Many of my clients are drunk or not thinking correctly, and when the police ask to see some ID, they actually pull out the fake ID by mistake or open their wallet to show the police the contents of the wallet, and the cop sees multiple ID's. This causes major issues in terms of having a defense to having the ID. It also doesn't matter if it's an ID that would be otherwise valid (it's actually someone's real ID, but not yours) or it's a totally manufactured "fake" ID that has your real picture, but the ID itself is not valid.

I have a strong track record of keeping this Fake ID charge off my client's record along with the original MIP. It certainly takes a very proactive plan in order to put ourselves in a position to achieve that result, but it is very possible. Like MIP charges, my clients begin volunteer work immediately. My clients need to overcome the perception that they are going to simply get another fake ID, and try the same thing again.

Why should my client get a second chance? If we can highlight who you've been in the past, what you're doing in the present (being proactive), and where you're going in the future (a great career where you can't have a misdemeanor), you will earn a second chance.

Urinating in Public - Indecent Exposure

I talk to a lot of clients who are charged with an MIP or Open Intox in Ann Arbor, but also get charged with Urinating in Public (UIP). I also get a lot of clients who are only charged with Urinating in Public, which in Michigan is a misdemeanor offense.

The crime of Urinating in Public can be written up in many different ways. It may fall under state law with the Washtenaw County Prosecutor's Office , as "indecent exposure" which is considered a sex crime under certain circumstances. It can also be charged as a disorderly person offense, which is quite vague, but includes the language of "a disorderly person is also one that is engaged in indecent or obscene conduct in a public place. See the two examples below.

Indecent Exposure: The State of Michigan has a statute against "indecent exposure". MCL 750.335a states that a person shall not knowingly make any open or indecent exposure of his or her person or of the person of another. There is a 1 year / $1000 misdemeanor and a high court (treated in the nature of a felony) 2 year / $2000 misdemeanor. A sexually delinquent person can be punished for an indeterminate term, the minimum of which is 1 day and the maximum of which is life.

Disorderly Persons: Michigan also has a statute punishing disorderly persons, which references indecent exposure. Under MCL 750.167, a disorderly person is a person who is intoxicated in a public place and who is either endangering directly the safety of another person or of property or is acting in a manner that causes a public disturbance. A disorderly person is also one that is engaged in indecent or obscene conduct in a public place. Either one of these could apply to someone who urinates in public.

The offense of urinating in public can also be written up under a local ordinance in the City of Ann Arbor. No matter which law you're charged under, the judge will be Judge Valvo or Judge Hines.

It is more common to be written up for a UIP under the City of Ann Arbor law, and frankly much better than under State law. Although it's better, it's still a misdemeanor, and still has a very embarrassing name attached to it. This is not the type of crime you want to come up on a background check.

The offense of UIP is quite frequent in a college town setting as many college age kids are walking home from bars and peeing outside in public. It's also common during tailgate season as people don't want to wait to use a public bathroom with large crowds.

The offense of a UIP unlike an MIP cannot be taken under any "first offender" type of option, and it's a crime unlike an MIP, but I have been very successful in having these types of charges dismissed, because my client was willing to begin my proactive program and demonstrate they are a good natured person who simply did a dumb thing.

Self-imposed sanctions ahead of time can generally have this matter dismissed, but it is not as easy as you may think. My clients engage in proactive volunteer work, and if alcohol was involved (99 percent of the time), my client will engage in an alcohol education class.

The judge and prosecutor use their common sense, and understand the reason you committed this crime was because you were likely drunk and had to go to the bathroom; if you were sober this would not happen. This is exactly why we address the alcohol issue, as the use of alcohol lead to you breaking the law. By focusing on the root of the problem, we can forecast that going forward you likely won't do this again, and we can likely get this charge dismissed.

<u>Disorderly Conduct/Public Drunkenness or Disturbance</u>

This section encompasses a number of different charges that both the City of Ann Arbor and the Washtenaw County Prosecutor's Office charge a lot of people with. If you're acting poorly, causing a scene, not complying with others, and you give the cops a tough time, they are going to charge you with some sort of disorderly conduct offense. There's a crime to charge you with based on just about any type of behavior.

The police in Ann Arbor typically give you a chance to leave the scene, and if you don't listen, you'll be charged with something. If you're not leaving a business despite multiple requests, causing a scene or fighting, you're going to get charged with a misdemeanor.

When you appear in court with one of these many charges, it will be assumed you were drunk, and "acting like an asshole". I've worked with hundreds of clients who were causing scenes in bars, restaurants, and out on the street or sidewalk, and due to the use of alcohol didn't use their best judgment and just shut up and walk away.

Now that my client is in court and sober, they don't want to be judged on that drunk moment, but why should a prosecutor or judge give you a break? Your past won't save, because you still acted in this manner despite past accomplishments. Your future goals might save you, but you should have reminded yourself of those goals when the police officer gave you a final chance to move on. The best way to avoid being judged on this one moment is by being proactive in the present. Together we offset this embarrassing moment by responding in a positive way, which demonstrates that you understand your actions, it's soaked in, and you've made changes going forward.

It's easy to say you're better than this moment, or you've learned from it; those are empty statements. It's what have you done since this moment in time to learn from it, and be better going forward?

Open Intoxicant/Container

This is by far the most common phone call that I receive in the fall, and usually during or after a football weekend. I hear from alumni who were back in town visiting, doctors, lawyers, moms, dads, fans of the opposing team, and people of every age, race and occupation. It all begins with the same phone call or email:

"This is ____________, I received a ticket for open container in Ann Arbor. I was tailgating/walking around with friends/going from one house to another, and the police stopped me, and told me I can't walk around with a beer"

The client then sometimes tells me they are from out of town, and they need to be in court in 10-14 days, and they don't know what to do.

The first thing I tell this client is that this ticket is a misdemeanor crime, and they need to call a timeout. Some potential clients are looking to get it over with as soon as possible; I tell these clients that if they plead guilty they will have a criminal record. Many people are shocked as this offense doesn't seem like a big deal or back home this isn't against the law. It's a huge wakeup call, and usually puts the client into panic mode.

I handle these cases in the same manner as I do other cases; we're proactive from day one. Although the case seems minor, we still need to treat is as major in the short term to avoid a long-term criminal record. I usually want to know everything I can about my client's career, and I request they send me a resume. I discuss issues they could have with a criminal record with their career, and we make a plan to have the misdemeanor dismissed. My clients cannot afford any other outcome for their job.

If my client is from the area, we attend court together; if my client is from out of town, I can usually work with the prosecutor and judge to have my client excused from court. If my client follows my lead with my proactive program, I can typically workout a dismissal with the judge and prosecutor, and keep a clean criminal record for my client.

If you're charged with with an open container offense in Ann Arbor, the prosecutor will usually be the City of Ann Arbor, and the judge will usually be Judge Valvo. Your case may be set with the magistrate at first, but we waive this court date, and get you a real court date where we can execute our plan, and have the case dismissed.

When we work together, you will no longer need to report to the courthouse within the 10-14 days listed on your ticket, because my attorney paperwork with satisfy this condition, and you will avoid a bench warrant. I will be able to take over all communication with the prosecutor and the judge, and we will formulate a comprehensive plan, set goals, and reach those goals together.

Another type of open intoxicant case happens in your vehicle. It is illegal in Michigan to have an open container in a vehicle. This is a misdemeanor offense, which can be found in the traffic code, and it cannot be expunged or dismissed as the original charge due to it being a traffic offense.

Anytime you combine a vehicle and alcohol, the next thought is drunk driving. Even if you haven't drank the beer, or you have, but you're under the legal limit, it only means the cops caught you in time before anything worse happened. This is exactly how a prosecutor and judge will view your case. We're proactive from day, and fill in all the unknowns with positive action.

We acknowledge that the case could have turned into a DUI, and combining alcohol use and a car are dangerous. It does not matter what the truth is, it's about the perception from the judge and prosecutor, which we're addressing. If we're proactive and address all possible concerns, we can usually work to a dismissal of charges, and no criminal record.

CHAPTER SEVEN

DRUNK DRIVING IN WASHTENAW COUNTY

According to the latest Michigan State Police Drunk Driving Audit, there were 850 DUI arrests in Washtenaw County. Of the 850 arrested, 609 were men, and 241 were women. These numbers don't tell the complete story of DUI offenses in Washtenaw County, because these numbers are always viewed in a worst case scenario point of view.

In the same time frame, there were 2,271 injuries caused by traffic accidents, and 23 deaths in Washtenaw County alone. While most DUI arrests don't involve a serious injury, or death, the prosecutor, judge and the community view this non-result to be lucky, rather than the logical outcome. When you're arrested and charged with a DUI in Washtenaw County, you'll be viewed as a dangerous drunk driver no matter how things ended on the road.

When a client contacts me about a DUI in Washtenaw County, they tell me about their family, their job, and all the responsibilities they have. Some clients are extremely remorseful about what happened, while some are already complaining about being arrested and charged, and want the case thrown out. While some cases do get dismissed and thrown out due to a problem with the violence or the actions of the police department, most cases are simply catching the person in the worst situation possible, drunk behind the wheel of their vehicle. People react very differently to feeling like they are not in control of their case, and their entire future is now at stake.

The first thing I do with any potential new client is call a timeout. Things are moving fast for the client, but moving very slow for me, because I handle hundreds of these cases each year. The client has usually never been arrested for anything, especially not drunk driving, and they need this timeout to re-focus on the process, and put together a game plan. I apply my mindset to my client, and we go over everything about the case, and about their own life.

It's important that I gain a full understanding of their life, and what lead up to this moment in time; I also need to know where they are heading in life with their goals and dreams. I'm quite blunt in telling the client that their past and future are relevant to our plan, but the prosecutor and the judge really don't care, because all of this was in place when you were arrested.

An example being the following: the client tells me that he drives a company car for a living, and must go jobsite to jobsite, along with domestic and international travel on a weekly basis, and he "cannot afford a DUI on his record".

My first response is that nobody wants a DUI on their record, and although you have some additional circumstances that make having a DUI conviction bad for your life and career, you seem to understand the consequences, and likely knew them before you put yourself in a bad position with the law. I'm blunt about this to my client, because he/she needs to understand how the judge and prosecutor sees the case. If you had all of that on the line, why would you even risk putting yourself in this situation?

Once we're clear on that perception, we can get to work on putting my client in a position where he/she has real power. A client does not have leverage or a bargaining position based on something that was in place when the offense occurred, but they can take complete control of their case in the present moment with a proactive program. The past and the future don't empower a client, but the present can.

I discuss my proactive program in great detail earlier in this book; for now, I want to focus on the inside the courtroom plan, and some specifics about each court in the County. Each DUI case in Washtenaw County has two paths; the proactive empowerment path where a client could earn a dismissal, a reduction and participate in determining their own outcome/sentence, and the path of contesting the charges for a dismissal or a not guilty verdict.

My clients go down both paths, until we have created all realistic outcomes based on the specific facts of their case. Here is my process, which I call the Information Gathering Stage.

Information Gathering Stage - DUI Charges in Washtenaw County

I'm going to go through this how I would go through a DUI consultation with a potential client charged with a DUI in Washtenaw County. I will also provide my insight into each aspect, and I go through the questions. This ten-step information gathering process was created based on my years as a prosecutor in both New York City and Michigan, and specifically what I've gathered working with different judges and prosecutors in the Washtenaw County.

#1 - I ask the client their age, their job/career, family situation.

I need to know these things, because I need to go inside the mind of the prosecutor and the judge. Being older is generally better for a DUI case, and having a good stable job with a family is good for bond conditions in terms of ties to the community; being married with children is usually better than being single with no kids when charged with a DUI in Washtenaw County.

#2 - I ask the client about their criminal history, and if they have ever been arrested and charged with anything in the past.

Obviously a past DUI offense is relevant in the current case along with any other alcohol or drug offense. An isolated non drug or alcohol conviction is not going to be as relevant, but a long criminal history will be very relevant as the judge and prosecutor see this offense as a long pattern with no end in sight. Jail becomes likely with a long criminal record. If the client has two or more DUI convictions, the case will likely be a felony, but begin at the 14A-1 District Court, before proceeding to the 22nd Circuit COurt.

#3 - We discuss where exactly this happened, what police department was involved, and if they were brought to a hospital or police department.

This helps me determine which court in Washtenaw County the case will be held, and which prosecutor and judge will be handling the case. By determining hospital vs police station, it gives me insight on the timetable for criminal charges as a blood test takes some time to come back for charges.

It also lets me know which police department I will need to contact in order to obtain the police reports, testing logs, test results, audio, video and other records created by your case. Some departments require FOIA requests, some don't, so it's important to know which department we're going to have to contact.

#4 - We discuss how the police came in contact with the client: accident, traffic stop, while sitting idle in a parking lot or parked on the side of the road, and if they were seen in the driver's seat or elsewhere.

If your case involved a traffic stop, we're going to need to take a timeout and evaluate the legitimacy of the stop . If an accident was involved, there might be medical records to review, and it's likely the EMS, fire department and additional police officers were involved who wrote reports, and may have their audio and video.

It may sound silly, but if nobody saw you behind the wheel of the car, the prosecutor still needs to prove you were driving, and that is not always as easy as you may think. I've been a prosecutor and a defense lawyer in many of these types of cases where the case went to trial on this very issue.

#5 - The potential client and I then discuss what they may have said to the police about, such as where they were going from, what they had to drink, and statements about driving.

Most DUI cases in Washtenaw County are traffic stops where the cop sees you driving, but if they don't, and you tell them you were driving then you've lost a possible defense. You also don't need to tell the cop you drank anything, but 95 percent of potential clients admit to drinking alcohol to the police officer. The client also usually tells the truth about where they were coming from, such as a bar, restaurant or party, which is fine, but it doesn't help your case.

Another underrated element of DUI cases in Washtenaw County is the timetable of alcohol consumption. Cops are trying to pinpoint your timetable, so they can document it in their police reports, and prevent your attorney from making arguments about rising blood, mouth alcohol, and the creative defense of "drinking after driving". If they can lock you down to your answer you while flustered, and not thinking about possible defenses, you lock yourself in more than you need to at the scene.

#6 - We then discuss what happens once outside the car - what field sobriety tests were performed, how did you do, and did you take a portable breath test.

Once outside the car, there may be a camera recording everything, which may give us an objective viewpoint of everything, but at this point, I need to know what you remember.

Most police reports in Washtenaw County read as if the client failed every test, slurring their speech etc; the perfect drunk driver to prosecute. Usually that is not true, but some elements of the officer's observations although subjective are likely true. At this point I am looking at the officer's basis for arresting you. Based on the tests you performed, his/her observations of you, did the officer have enough to place you under arrest, and if not, should everything thereafter the bad arrest be suppressed, and your case dismissed?

I am also looking to see what your blood alcohol content (BAC) was at the scene. Although not admissible at trial (although admissible in very limited circumstances), it gives us an idea of where your BAC was going (up or down) when we compare it to the later result. It also gives the prosecutor strong evidence to show the arrest was valid if the BAC is or above 0.08.

#7 - We then discuss the point when you were arrested, and if you were read any rights, which relate to statements or chemical test rights.

For DUI cases in Washtenaw County, most of the incriminating statements are made during the "investigation phase" while standing at the car, or while performing tests. For the most part, you are not yet in custody and/or under arrest, and statements made at this point likely don't require *Miranda* rights.

As for chemical test rights, sometimes the officer reads them at the time of arrest, or in the car on the way to the police station. I will want to know if they were read, and what you recall the circumstances at the time.

Audio and video evidence may be available to learn more about this stage of the case. This could be an in-car device, or a recording device at the police station, otherwise known as a bookin video.

#8 - Assuming you're brought to the police station, we will discuss observation time, and the DataMaster test.

In Michigan, the police must observe you for 15 minutes prior to administering the DataMaster test. If this does not occur, the results can be suppressed via motion or challenged at trial. If you believe you threw up, coughed excessively or put something in your mouth before the test, I need to know this, because it could impact the results.

The DataMaster is the machine used in Michigan for chemical breath tests, and typically two tests are administered. Generally, if only one test was done, or one of the tests had an issue, that may be a fruitful exploration for dismissal or a defense at trial. This ins and outs of the challenging the DataMaster are discussed in far greater detail in my other books and my websites if you would like to review.

During this time, the officer should have read you the chemical test rights if they have not done so already. You have the option to refuse the breath test, but the officer SHOULD inform you of the consequences, such as suspension of license for a year and 6 points on your driving record.

#9 - If you end up having blood drawn, we will discuss how you got there, and the impact on your case

If the officer takes you to the hospital by his/her choice or you go via ambulance (more likely in accident cases), and blood is drawn, this will delay your case as we wait for results. If the officer wanted to do the DataMaster test, but you refused, we will discuss the Implied Consent issues triggered, and your options.

If you refuse the DataMaster in Washtenaw County, you have 14 days to send in the paperwork for an appeal; if not, your license is gone and you have six points on your license. The Implied Consent process and the hardship license option is beyond the scope of this book, and available in my other books, and my website for your review.

#10 - The final conversation is about possible court dates, and beginning my proactive plan immediately.

Some clients already have a court date when they contact me, but some are still waiting for a court date. Some clients have a ticket, which says they must contact the court within X amount of days. Either way, if we decide to work together, we will likely call a timeout and have this first court date waived or adjourned. Beyond going through these steps, we now need to acquire all of the evidence, which the prosecutor and judge already have in their possession. We need to get on an even playing field as we explore all possible defenses.

We also need to begin my proactive program, which will be geared to the specific facts of your case, and take into consideration the assigned judge and prosecutor. Ideally, I like to create about a 30-day window.

The In's and Out's of Washtenaw County DUI Charges

As we've discussed numerous times in this book, the court is determined by the location of the offense, and the prosecutor is determined by the type of charge and the police department involved.

According to a Michigan State Police study, the Washtenaw County Sheriff's Office was responsible for 229 DUI arrests, while the Michigan State Police made 168 arrests. Right there that's 397 DUI cases that MUST be handled by the Washtenaw County Prosecutor's Office.

Along with these arrests, any second, third or subsequent DUI charge, and any felony must go to the County. You also have the University of Michigan Police Department with 45 of their own arrests, along with Eastern Michigan Police Department with 11 arrests, all which go through the County.

When these numbers are added up, more than half of all the DUI arrests in Washtenaw County will be charged by the County. Generally speaking the County level negotiates less, and if they do, it's going to take an aggressive proactive plan to move the needle to create multiple options in your case.

In addition, approximately 28 percent of DUI cases in Washtenaw County are blood draws, which delays more than a quarter of the cases in the County. Of this 28 percent, approximately 12 percent are refusal cases, which mean the client faces that 14-day appeal window before losing their license for a year, and having 6 points on their license regardless of the outcome of their criminal case.

Washtenaw County DUI Cases by Court & Judge

Here is a brief overview of the current judges, prosecutors and breakdown of DUI charges by district court:

#1 - 15th District Court - Ann Arbor

All drunk driving cases at the 15th District Court are currently handled by Judge Joseph Burke. The main police departments that make DUI arrests for the Ann Arbor District Court are the Washtenaw County Sheriff's Office, the Ann Arbor Police Department (126 arrests), and the University of Michigan Police Department (45 arrests) for a total of around 200 DUI arrests and charges (both misdemeanor and felony charges).

The Washtenaw County Prosecutor's Office handles all of the felony DUI charges, and the arrests made by the Sheriff's Office, but the most frequent prosecutor at the 15th District Court is the City of Ann Arbor Attorney, who could handles the misdemeanor DUI arrests made by the Ann Arbor Police Department.

#2 - 14A-1 District Court - Pittsfield Township

The Pittsfield Township District Court is handled by Judge Richard Conlin, who presides over every misdemeanor drunk driving case. The main police departments making arrests in the area are the Washtenaw County Sheriff's Office, the Michigan State Police and the Pittsfield Township Police Department (153 arrests).

The Washtenaw County Prosecutor's Office handles all of the felony DUI charges, and the arrests made by the Sheriff's Office and the Michigan State Police, while the Pittsfield Township Prosecutor handles all the misdemeanor arrests made by the Pittsfield Township Police Department.

#3 - 14A-2 District Court - City of Ypsilanti

The City of Ypsilanti District Court is handled by Judge Kirk W. Tabbey, who presides over every misdemeanor drunk driving case. The main police departments making arrests in the area are the Washtenaw County Sheriff's Office, the Michigan State Police, the Ypsilanti Police

Department (41 arrests), and the Eastern Michigan Police Department (11 arrests).

The Washtenaw County Prosecutor's Office handles all of the felony DUI charges, and the arrests made by the Sheriff's Office, Michigan State Police and the Eastern Michigan PD, while the City of Ypsilanti Prosecutor handles all the misdemeanor arrests made by the Ypsilanti Police Department.

#4 - 14A-3 District Court - Chelsea

The Chelsea District Court is handled by Judge Richard Conlin, who presides over every misdemeanor drunk driving case. The main police departments making arrests in the area are the Washtenaw County Sheriff's Office, the Michigan State Police, Northfield Township Police Department (22 arrests), and the Chelsea Police Department (9 arrests).

The Chelsea District Court is unique in that the Washtenaw County Prosecutor's Office handles the majority of DUI cases, because the Sheriff's Office and the Michigan State Police make up the majority of the arrests for this court.

The Washtenaw County Prosecutor's Office handles all of the felony DUI charges, and the arrests made by the Sheriff's Office and the Michigan State Police, while the Northfield Township and Chelsea cases are handled by their respective prosecutors.

#5 - 14A-4 District Court - Saline

The Saline District Court is handled by Judge Cedric Simpson, who presides over every misdemeanor drunk driving case. The main police departments making arrests in the area are the Washtenaw County Sheriff's Office, the Milan Police Department (4 arrests), and the Saline Police Department (42 arrests).

The Washtenaw County Prosecutor's Office handles all of the felony DUI charges, and the arrests made by the Sheriff's Office, while the Milan and Saline cases are handled by their respective prosecutors.

#6 - 14-B District Court - Ypsilanti Township

The 14-B District Court handles around 130-150 DUI cases each year. Judge Charles Pope presides over all of the misdemeanor cases in Ypsilanti Township, and the main arresting police agencies are the Washtenaw County Sheriff's Department and Michigan State Police.

The Washtenaw County Prosecutor's Office handles all of the felony DUI charges, and the arrests made by these arresting agencies.

CHAPTER EIGHT

FREQUENTLY ASKED QUESTIONS

This final chapter is meant to cover topics and specific questions that I typically receive from potential clients about their Washtenaw County case. The easiest way to break this down is a simple Question & Answer format. If I haven't addressed your question throughout this book or in this section, I encourage you to reach out to me, and address the specific topic or question with me.

Q. I'm being investigated for a crime in Washtenaw County, but not charged - what does this mean? This means that the police department is still gathering information on your case. Once the investigation is completed, the information will be turned over to the prosecutor who will determine whether or not to charge you with a crime. The police department may have an influence over the charges, but the final decision is made by the prosecutor.

Cases that are "investigated" are typically cases being reviewed at the County level, whereas the local level, cases are presented and prosecuted with far less investigation.

Q. What's a Pretrial - does this mean I'm going to trial? A pretrial is exactly what it sounds like; it's the court appearance before a trial. You may have 2, 3 or 8 pretrials, and may or may not have a trial at all. From my experience, about 2 percent of all cases actually go to trial, the other 98 percent are resolved prior to going to trial. If you're charged with a misdemeanor, your first court appearance is likely to be a pretrial if the arraignment is waived or combined.

Q. Will I be charged with a misdemeanor or felony? This decision will be made by the prosecutor who will be provided the case information by the police department. If the facts fit a felony crime, then a prosecutor will usually charge you with the highest possible offense. Prosecutors do this to create leverage in negotiation, and may ultimately agree to settle the case for a misdemeanor.

All felonies in Washtenaw County are charged by the Washtenaw County Prosecutor's office. If for example the prosecutor is the City of Ann Arbor or Pittsfield Township, your case will be a misdemeanor.

Q. I was arrested weeks ago in Washtenaw County, but not charged yet - what's going on? This is a very common occurrence in Washtenaw County. An arrest conducted by the police department does not automatically create a criminal charge. The case must be reviewed by the prosecutor before someone is charged. For many misdemeanors, and some felonies there will be a delay between the arrest and the charge. This is VERY common for drunk driving crimes, and drug offenses where the evidence must be tested at the Michigan State Police Lab.

Q. The police want to talk to me about my case - what should I do? You have a constitutional right to remain silent, and this silence cannot be used against you. The police may act like your friend, but they have a job to do, and that job is to gather incriminating evidence, which will assist the prosecutor in charging you with a crime. Even if you have nothing to hide, you may not realize that your statement could incriminate you. The police are not looking to help you or cut you a break; they do not keep their jobs by letting people off the hook.

Ask to speak to an attorney before uttering one word to the police department. If you've already talked to the police, we can't take back what you said, but if you were not made aware of your rights, we may be able to have the statements suppressed.

A lot of times, in Washtenaw County, the police submit a case to the prosecutor, but the prosecutor doesn't have enough to charge, and they "further" the case for additional investigation. If the police contact you down the road, they are acting on behalf of the prosecutor to strengthen their case by talking to you. If you keep your mouth closed, you prevent charges; talk without a lawyer and you may have just added the final piece to the puzzle.

Q. What's an arraignment? In Washtenaw County, this will be your first court appearance where you appear before a magistrate or judge. You do not have the right to an attorney at this point in your case; you must hire an attorney to be represented at your arraignment.

The magistrate or judge will read the charges and you will enter a plea of not-guilty, guilty or stand mute. The magistrate or judge will also set a bond, along with various bond conditions. I would advise anyone charged with a crime to hire an attorney for an arraignment. If you hire an attorney, you will likely be able to skip this court date in Washtenaw County. If not skip it entirely, it will be moved back in time to be combined with your first pretrial.

Q. If the judge sets a bond in my case, how do I pay? A judge can set a personal recognizance bond, which means you simply promise to return to court, but don't post any money. A judge may also set a cash or surety bond, which means you will need to post this amount to be released during the pendency of your case.

If the judge sets a 10 percent provision, it means you only need to actually post 10 percent of the amount set, and the other 90 percent will be owed to the court if you do not show-up. It is always best to bring someone to post bond for you, because some courts may not allow a defendant to post their own bond.

Most misdemeanors in Washtenaw County, and some felonies do receive personal bonds if you have an attorney present, and have demonstrated proactive steps since the incident. An example would be attending AA or seeing a counselor before even appearing in court.

Q. Will the police come to my house and arrest me? If you've been charged with a crime in Washtenaw County, the police can come arrest you based upon an an active arrest warrant. Most of the courts in Washtenaw County will not issue an arrest warrant for a misdemeanor, but will always do so for a felony.

For felony offenses in Washtenaw County, the police will most likely come arrest you, unless your attorney can arrange to have a walk-in arraignment to avoid an embarrassing arrest. If you are charged with a misdemeanor, you will receive a notice in the mail to appear for court or you were already issued a ticket, and will most likely not be arrested prior to this court date.

In Washtenaw County, all felony arraignments happen at the 14A-1 Service Center next to the jail. If you are arrested on the warrant, you will be arraigned in handcuffs and a jumpsuit. If you hired an attorney and voluntarily come in with your lawyer, you will see the magistrate without being in custody, and likely receive either a personal bond or a very manageable bond to post.

Q. Can I get my court date moved back in Washtenaw County? This depends upon the court, the individual judge and the stage of your case. Most judges in Washtenaw County are flexible with granting at least one court adjournment, but this will be more difficult if you're trying to move your case without the assistance of an attorney.

Judges in Washtenaw County have timing requirements to resolve cases, and are not willing to risk their own reputation to fit your schedule. Having an attorney speak to the prosecutor (who must agree) and the judge about the reasons for moving the court date are likely to be successful.

Q. What if I can't go to the court on my scheduled date? If you don't appear for court in Washtenaw County, a bench warrant will be issued for your arrest, and you could forfeit any bond posted. It is always best to try to make arrangements to move your court date rather than not showing up.

Not appearing for court could also jeopardize any plea agreements or sentencing agreements, which were negotiated on your behalf. When you don't show up for court, your credibility and your truthfulness are quickly put in jeopardy, and you are likely to be jailed.

Q. I've never committed a crime before, does the prosecutor care? Your criminal history and background could play a major role in the outcome of your case. That being said, the prosecutor does not focus much on individual cases, but it's not because the prosecutor is a bad person or has no heart.

Prosecutor's deal with thousands of criminal defendants each year, and don't have the time or patience to decide who deserves special treatment or even a second chance. It's up to your attorney to present your history and background in the most favorable way.

Criminal record or no criminal record, being proactive from day one is the best way in my opinion to make the prosecutor "care" about you, or give you any special positive attention. Fortunately for clients in Washtenaw County, there are a lot of really good prosecutors, who will take the time to hear about my clients, and what they have been doing proactively since the incident and arrest.

Q. What if the victim wants to drop the charges in Washtenaw County- will my case be dismissed? There's a major misconception that the victim makes the decision to prosecute. This is not true; a victim is merely a witness who provides factual information to the police department or prosecutor. Based upon this information, an arrest or investigation will occur, and the prosecutor will charge someone on behalf of the State of Michigan or the city of township they represent. The defendant has committed a crime against the State, of Michigan in violation of a law rather than an individual person.

The most common type of case, which this question arises is a domestic violence case. The Washtenaw County Prosecutor's Office will not drop the charge no matter how many times the victim makes the request. In their eyes, the victim is attempting to drop the charge in the best interest of the person charged rather than themselves.

Q. Does the victim need to hire their own attorney to prosecute me? No, the prosecutor will prosecute the case on behalf of the People of the State of Michigan or the city of township they represent. The victim is not a party to the case; the victim is considered a factual witness who may provide testimony or receive restitution. Occasionally the victim in a case will hire an attorney to advise them as to their rights, and options if the prosecutor should subpoena them to court. The victim may also want to hire an attorney to file a civil suit alleging damages. But for the actual prosecution, the victim works with the prosecutor, not their own lawyer.

Q. How much does it cost to hire a lawyer? It depends upon what crime you're charged with, and where your case is pending. Lawyers charge all different prices for different cases. Whenever a client contacts me, I let them immediately that if they are shopping based on price alone, then they are wasting their time by talking to me.

I explain that hiring an attorney for your Washtenaw County case is not like buying a flat screen television, and shopping the Costco, Target and Amazon sales; the attorneys are not all the same; they couldn't be any different in their experience, game plans and the options that they can create for your case.

I encourage clients to do their research, and find out what makes each attorney unique. In my view there are about 500 attorneys you could hire in Washtenaw County, and many of those attorneys can put on a suit, go to court, and tell you how your case will be resolved. If you're looking for a cattle call outcome like everyone else, those attorneys would likely be able to live up to your expectations. Using the television analogy, for the most part, all of the these attorneys will "turn on and work", but if you want more than a flickering screen, you will dig deeper into your research, and demand more.

When a client asks me what makes my approach unique for a Washtenaw County case, I have them review my proactive plan in great detail, and discuss my experience and insight practicing in the County on a daily basis. I then encourage them to read this book, and ask the other lawyers they are considering if they've written a book about Washtenaw County; there's usually a lot of silence from the other lawyers to that inquiry.

Q. Should I use the public defender in Washtenaw County? If you're asking yourself this question, then I think you already know the answer. There are different levels of attorneys who could be assigned your case, and you will not get to pick your lawyer, which is not how I would proceed with the most crucial moment in my life. It's like getting married, and being handed your dress or suit at the last minute with no input or opportunity to make alterations. Even worse, it's an arranged marriage without your family or anyone else having any input on your suitor.

In my opinion, unless you're charged with a headline grabbing felony, a public defender cannot give you the time and attention you need during the most challenging time in your life. I'm going to leave it at that in terms of the why not, and instead focus on why you should make every effort to hire your own attorney.

I can't speak for other attorneys, but when you hire me, you're getting my unlimited time, open line of communication, and most importantly my proactive program. You also need to like your attorney, and be confident in the game plan you've put together, rather than being told how things are going to happen. While I don't make it into a nightly practice, I've exchanged emails, texts and calls with current and potential clients at one in the morning. A quick look at my past client reviews will back up my accessibility to clients. Good luck getting the public defender to respond after 4:30 or on the weekend or holiday.

I've never run into a client who had the ability to hire their own attorney, and they instead went with the public defender. If you don't have the money, and you use the public offender, the court is still going to bill you for using them; there is nothing free about a public defender.

If you don't have the money, borrow money from a family member or friend. Being charged with a crime is not the time to be frugal and hope everything works out. If you only have some money now, with the expectation you'll have more later, I do occasionally agree to payment plans.

Q. Will the judge care that I'm a good person? Judges will know very little about you during your case. The judge is not in a position to distinguish between the good people and the bad people. The judge will get a first impression based on your appearance and your speech, but it's up to your attorney to add additional detail.

This additional information is provided by your proactive efforts; the steps you have taken since this incident occurred. Your past and future are not as relevant to a judge, as words are easy to use; judges see thousands of cases each year, and your case is not as unique as you think it is. What's unique to a judge, is taking proactive steps outside the courtroom, and coming to court with real achievements, that are highly relevant your present case.

Q. Should I tell the truth to my attorney? Absolutely! Your attorney is obligated to keep all conversations and information confidential. If you don't tell your attorney the truth then your attorney is defending you with one hand tied behind his/her back. It's quite common for a client to leave out important details, and the attorney is put in a bad position or surprised when the information is made available. It may be too late to recover from this lack of open and honest communication.

You should be truthful with your attorney about your past, the facts of your case, and any developments along the way. Some clients think that if they tell their attorney one story, then somehow that will become the truth, and help their case. If you have facts that hurt your case, your attorney will not disclose those facts, but may be able navigate around them. If your attorney doesn't know the truth, and it comes out in another manner, your attorney will not have the opportunity to plan how to best address this information.

Q. Can I bring my phone to the court house? Most courthouses in Washtenaw County do not allow any electronic devices including cell phones. Some court houses have lockers to put phones, but other courthouses do not provide this accommodations. It is best to leave your phone in the car or at home. If you need to make a phone call while at the courthouse, you will have access to a public phone.

As of the publishing of this book, the 14A-3 Court in Chelsea and the 14A-2 and 14B District Courts in Ypsilanti allow phones in the building; the others do not allow non-lawyers and other exempt parties from bringing in a cell phone.

Q. What will happen at my Preliminary Examination? If charged with a felony in Washtenaw County, you have the right to a Preliminary Examination before reaching the 22nd Washtenaw Circuit Court. There are three different things that can happen. The examination will be held where the prosecuting attorney must show probable cause that a crime was committed, and that you committed the crime. The examination could be waived, meaning that the case will go to the Washtenaw Circuit Court without an examination. The final option is the case is resolved with a plea as charged, or to reduced charges. The preliminary examination is the gatekeeper to felony charges in Washtenaw County.

Q. Will I be drug tested by the court or probation in Washtenaw County? Yes, you can be tested by order of the judge or by probation. It's quite common for a judge to ask whether or not you will pass a drug test; depending upon your answer, the judge may test you on the spot. It is always best to be honest, because lying to a judge is never a good thing.

Probation can and will subject you to random and scheduled drug testing. If you fail a drug test, you could be in violation of your bond conditions, your probation terms, or be charged with a new crime.

In Washtenaw County, monitoring and testing for drugs and alcohol go through the Washtenaw County Community Corrections. According to their website:

"Community Corrections is provides State and locally funded jail and prison diversion programs and sanctioning options for eligible persons at all stages of the criminal justice process. Our role is to reduce the potential to re-offend and to support the safe and appropriate reintegration of offenders into our communities. A collaborative, community-based initiative, we emphasize comprehensive, integrated programs and services that act as an integral part of the Sheriff's Office mission of creating public safety, providing quality service and building strong and sustainable communities."

Q. Will the police officer be at my court date in Washtenaw County? Usually not, but if your case is set for a hearing on a traffic ticket, an evidentiary hearing or a trial, the officer will be present in court. On occasion a police officer will attend your arraignment and give his/her opinion on bond. Most people believe the police ar always the enemy, but they are doing their job, and can actually be a strong advocate for you.

Many people assume that if a police officer does not show up for court, then the case is dismissed. This is not true but for some traffic ticket hearings, and even then, the prosecutor can have the officer re-issue the ticket. The police departments in Washtenaw County are generally very good about showing up for court compared to other counties in the area.

Q. How many times will I need to go to court? Court cases in Washtenaw County can last anywhere from one to ten plus court dates. At a minimum you will need to attend court for an arraignment, which could be combined with a pre-trial conference. Unless you are sentenced the same day, most cases are take a minimum of two court appearances. You should not be in a rush to get the case over it; you should listen to your attorney, and proceed with the goal of obtaining the best result, not the quickest result.

Q. What's the difference between jail and prison? If you are not released on bond, you will sit in the Washtenaw County Jail during the pendency of your case. If you are to serve less than one year on a felony or misdemeanor, then you go to a Washtenaw County Jail to serve your sentence, which is located on Hogback and Washtenaw in Pittsfield Township.

If you are sentenced to more than a year on a felony you go to prison, which is run by the Michigan Department of Corrections. You would serve time in a prison, which is outside of Washtenaw County. In sum, it is far better to go to jail than to go to prison, because you have a determinate date versus prison, which does not have a set release date.

Q. Can I travel during my case in Washtenaw County? In order to travel during your Washtenaw County case, both the prosecutor and the judge must agree. This request is usually granted on most misdemeanors and felonies, but it really depends upon your charge, your criminal history, and where you want to travel.

It is more likely you will be granted permission to leave the State of Michigan rather than the country, but both are possible. If you are currently under court order for drug and/or alcohol, or have other monitoring, your attorney should be prepared to suggest an alternative method to accomplish this monitoring. For alcohol, your attorney can usually talk to the judge into allowing a portable alcohol monitoring device, or information about alternative means to test.

Q. What does discovery mean? In a criminal case, this means all the paperwork and evidence in possession of the police department and prosecutor. There may be additional discovery from a third party such as a hospital, bank or pawn shop to name a few.

The main piece of discovery is the police report. The discovery process is ongoing, and new information may become available during the pendency of your case. I call this the Information Gathering Stage, which I discussed earlier in this book. Depending on the charge the client may know little to nothing about the evidence being used against them by the prosecutor.

The different police agencies and prosecutors in the County are pretty good about turning things over, but each has their own requirements and best practices to put into place to receive what we need in a timely manner.

Q. What's a prosecutor? The prosecutor is a representative of the state, county, city or township that has brought charges against you. You could be dealing with an elected prosecutor of a county such as the Washtenaw County Prosecutor's Office, or a local prosecutor like the City of Ann Arbor. In Washtenaw County, the current prosecutor is Brian Mackie who is elected, and he has around 20-25 assistant prosecutors handling the cases in the County. Many of the city or townships have a small law firm handling their cases or even sometimes a single person.

Q. Is a magistrate the same thing as a judge in Washtenaw County? A magistrate generally attends to arraignments and traffic offenses. If you're arraigned on a new charge, you may appear before a magistrate rather a judge. A magistrate is not elected like a judge, but they have incredible power to affect the course of your case. You should show a magistrate the same respect as a judge, and address them as "your honor".

In Washtenaw County, the Ann Arbor District Court has it's own magistrate that works in conjunction with the three judges. The 14A courts in Pittsfield Township, Ypsilanti, Chelsea and Saline has their own sets of magistrates that rotate in and out of those courts, and the 14-B District Court has its own magistrate.

Q. Can I bring a friend or family member to court? Yes, the courtroom is open to the general public, so you can bring anyone to court for support. Having a friend or family member in court can be very comforting to a client.

Now is it necessary to have a family or friend in court? No it is not. A lot of parents call me and ask whether they should fly in for court appearances; while it is certainly allowed, it is not always necessary.

Having a friend or family member in court will usually have no impact on your charges, but can help at sentencing if a judge sees that others are supporting you, and will assist in getting you on the right path once your time in court is over. A younger client may receive less monitoring if a judge knows that a parent(s) is involved and invested.

Q. How long will I have a criminal record? Some crimes cannot be removed from your criminal record (traffic offenses including drunk driving). Some offenses can be expunged off of your record after five years, as long as you meet other requirements. If you're a first offender, there are a number of opportunities to keep a charge from appearing on your record from day one, which if you successfully complete the terms of your sentence, you will not have a criminal record. These opportunities must be earned, and both the prosecutor and the judge must agree that this is an outcome that you deserve.

It's also important to note that receiving the consideration on a "first offender" type deal is only the first step. It's like being admitted into a school, because you still need to graduate from the program. A judge can set you up for failure over the next 12-24 months and any slipups results in the charge being on your record, and you will likely go right to jail.

Q. Am I ever going to get a job? If you're charged with a crime, or are ultimately convicted of a crime, this could affect your ability to keep a job, or get a new job. Certain crimes like drunk driving could affect your ability to drive a vehicle. A conviction for assault or domestic violence can be particularly troubling for gaining future employment. The biggest barrier to obtaining employment is a felony conviction.

Because your case can impact your career, it's important to discuss these concerns from day one, and put the right plan into place. For example if you're a nurse, you cannot have a retail fraud or a drug conviction on your record, or if you're a commercial truck driver, a DUI conviction will take away your CDL and cost you a job.

Q. Where's the courthouse? If you are scheduled for court then the court house address should be listed on the appearance notice. If not, you can put the name of the court into Google, and you will be provided with the address.

Don't get the 15th District Court at 301 East Huron and the 22nd Circuit Court at 101 East Huron confused. The Circuit Court is where you go on felony cases, the 15th District Court handles misdemeanors. Another easy point of confusion are the 14A-2 and 14B courts in Ypsilanti.

I've also seen clients get confused when it comes to their Preliminary Examination Conferences, which all take place at the 14A-1 District Court on Hogback & Washtenaw. If you're charged with a felony, you will always go to this court, and NOT the District Court in the area where this incident happened.

Q. What should I wear to court? You should dress like you're going on a professional job interview. You only get to make a first impression once; the judge and prosecutor will be looking at your attire. Our goal is to change the perception of your case with the prosecutor and the judge, and if you come to court looking like an average Joe or Jane, then that's how you'll be treated.

We will discuss the specifics of what you should wear for court. Your attire should be an asset to resolving your case in a favorable way, not a hinder to success. If you wear a uniform for work, and you're either coming from work, or going to work, we will discuss if it's worth bringing a change of clothing depending upon your case.

Q. Will I have to speak in court? For arraignment and pretrial court dates, you will have to say very little in court. Be prepared to state your name for the official court record and "yes your honor" and "no your honor". If you're pleading to a charge or being sentenced, then I will prepare you for what you will need to say.

The only time you will speak more than a few sentences is if your case goes to trial, and you take the witness stand in your own defense.

General rule for my clients is they don't apologize for their actions; too many clients who are represented by other lawyers apologize to the judge, which makes no sense. My client did not do anything to the judge; they were likely sleeping or at their daughter's softball game when you were arrested.

My clients discuss the impact the case has had on their life, what they have done in response to this case, what they have learned, and the tools they have in place going forward in life.

Q. How long will my court date last in Washtenaw County? Most people are surprised to find out that a court appearance is 95 percent waiting and 5 percent action. If your case is set for 1 pm, you might not have your case called until 2:30 pm. Once your case is called, unless there is a hearing or a trial, you will stand before the judge from anywhere between 30 seconds and 8 minutes. A lot of the negotiation and discussion happens prior to or after your case happens.

I make it a habit to be the first attorney present in the courtroom. I want to talk to the prosecutor first, and get our case first on the list to be called by the judge. I find it beneficial to clients to work with the prosecutor and the judge when they are fresh, and not worn out from other cases. It's also better for my client's job, and other responsibilities to limit time spent sitting around.

Q. Why did my lawyer go speak to the judge without me? This is called a bench conference where your attorney may want to speak to the judge and prosecutor without making a record. Some things are better discussed outside of the ear of the public, and not on an official court record in Washtenaw County.

Good plea deals, favorable sentences, and strong advocacy happens at the bench. This is not something to be worried about. I will usually warn my clients that I will be approaching the bench with the prosecutor, so they are not taken by surprise when it happens.

Q. Am I going to jail or prison? Most first offenders who commit misdemeanor offenses do not go to jail. Jail is in place to punish offenders who are not suitable for the alternative sentence of probation. From day one, my client is on a proactive plan to put themselves in the education/learn from it column, and avoid the punishment column. Probation is a privilege, not a right, and the client must earn this result.

The goal is to preview the distinction for the prosecutor and judge with my proactive program, and head down the right path from day one. Better to have the judge and prosecutor agree to what we want and support us, than to actively jump in with their own solution, because they are not convinced the client has learned anything from the experience.

If you're charged with a felony, then all bets are off; Michigan felonies are subject to the Michigan sentencing guidelines. Certain felonies have mandatory jail or prison, which cannot be avoided. If you're a first offender or committed a lower level felony offense, jail is still quite possible, but less likely. Even the most serious felony offenses can be mitigated by being proactive from day one.

Q. Is my case going to be a trial? Most cases in Washtenaw County do not go to trial, but going to trial is not something to fear. If you've been charged with a crime, and the facts do not meet the elements of the offense, then a trial may be appropriate in your case. You can have a trial by judge or jury. Each type of trial has it's relative strengths and weaknesses.

All of my clients in Washtenaw County are presented with their trial options. We discuss different defenses, and the pros and cons of each approach. These defenses are a result of the information gathering process, which begins on day one. I will only recommend a trial to the client if it is in their best interest, but ultimately the client decides if they want to go to trial or not.

Made in United States
Orlando, FL
04 November 2026

90202576R00075